D1643310

What readers are saying...

'I enjoyed this book so much. A wonderful collection of stories by women from different backgrounds, parts of the world and stages of life. I admire and appreciate the honesty they have brought to us through their experiences and the lessons they have learned along the way. Reminding me that we are all a work in progress. Life and the world can feel overwhelming at times. As women we so often take too much on our shoulders, we forget to stop and appreciate and yes, we can take life much too seriously. Through the insights shared beautifully through these stories, I have been reminded again and again that yes, this life of ours really is an "inside job", that we are here to thrive, learn and grow and the stories we tell ourselves will make all the difference to how that pans out for each of us.'

Julie Siddiqi MBE is a mentor, consultant and gender equality campaigner with a focus on interfaith relations and on applying that to social action work, together. She is also a regular contributor to BBC Radio 4's *Thought for the Day*

'A Life Less Serious *is a collection of sparkling, glowing, precious jewels. The contributions from these remarkable women all, through the uniqueness and exquisite variety of their own voices and experiences, point consistently to what lies beneath those voices and experiences. Shifting from laugh-out-loud funny to deeply moving from one line to another, it is truly a treasure trove of all human life. Open it, dive in and savour each word.'

Clare Dimond, author of *REAL: The Inside-Out Guide to Being Yourself* and other books in the REAL series

'The stories in A Life Less Serious *demonstrate how the world we each see is a projection of always-changing thought. As our identification with thought changes, the entire world changes. As we see thought as thought, life looks far less serious and as a result, much happier and more hopeful.*

'These stories show how we can be fully human, living in the midst of what appears to be a time full of serious circumstances, with more lightness and peace. Taking things less seriously isn't irresponsible and it's not impossible. Levity and joy are our true nature. This beautiful collection of stories shows how a life less serious is the most responsible, loving, natural way to be, and it is available to all of us.'

Amy Johnson PhD, author of *Just a Thought: A No-Willpower Approach to Overcome Self-Doubt and Make Peace with Your Mind* and *The Little Book of Big Change: The No-Willpower Approach to Breaking Any Habit*

'Have you ever found yourself sitting on a park bench, or an airplane seat, talking to a complete stranger, but finding that their life story unfolded effortlessly and you felt this incredible closeness to them... an acknowledgement of your shared humanity? You don't know them at all, but somehow you know them. Elements of their story are your story. The loneliness, the beauty, the struggle, the healing. This beautiful book reads like a collection of those kinds of experiences. Sometimes it's nice to read books written by "writers" or "philosophers" or "experts," but sometimes it's nicer to just hear the unpretentious, unpolished stories of our fellow beings. I found A Life Less Serious *to be like the closeness of spirit I've been missing and longing for in these strange pandemic-induced quiet times. Pour yourself a cup of tea or a glass of wine and enjoy the heartfelt truths that are so authentically shared by the women in these pages.*

Mara Gleason Olsen, Cofounder of the One Solution Foundation, a Chicago-based, globally active, non-profit, whose mission is to uncover human resilience and open hearts and minds

'Read one or two stories from A Life Less Serious *and you might be able to dismiss the women essayists as out to lunch or as unlike you. Read all of them and it's hard not to take them as – well, onto something! Each story describes how a psychospiritual understanding known as The Three Principles released love, joy, and wisdom from the writers' souls into their hearts and minds. Freer from seriousness, and in the lightness of those beautiful feelings, they brought needed spiritual medicine to relationships, work and to the world. Love and insight color every page.'*

Linda Sandel Pettit EdD, author and inspiratrix to healers

'Reading this book is like sitting with close friends while they share some of their most personal and challenging moments. Funny, heartfelt and refreshingly honest, you can't help but relate to their humanity. Each story is unique but they all point towards a deeper, universal truth about the human experience. Just a tiny glance of this truth can change your life for the better. Life can really test us but, even in the darkest moments, there is always light and it lives inside us all. If you want more light in your life, this book is for you.'

Chantal Burns, founder of the Conscious Leadership School and author of *Instant Motivation: The surprising truth behind what really drives top performance* and *Bulletproof: Be fearless and resilient, no matter what*

A Life Less Serious

Real life stories from women to inspire, uplift and encourage new perspectives on living

Edited by George Halfin

A Life Less Serious

Copyright 2022 © The Contributors of A Life Less Serious
ISBN 978-1-7397268-0-5
First published in Great Britain by My Light Publishing 2022

A catalogue record of this book is available from the British Library
Set and designed by The Book Refinery Ltd
Cover design and illustrations by Thoughts Make Things
Proofreading by Rachel Nixon of Accuracy Matters Ltd
Copy editing by George Halfin, Carol Boroughs and Lucy Sheffield

All rights reserved. No part of this publication may be reproduced, stored in a retrieval system, or transmitted in any form or by any means, electronic, mechanical, photocopying, recording or otherwise without the prior permission of the publishers and/or the writer(s) who wrote the piece(s).Worldwide copyright remains with the writer.

This book is sold subject to the condition that it shall not, by way of trade or otherwise, be lent, resold, hired out or otherwise circulated without the publisher's prior consent in any form of binding or cover other than that in which it is published and without a similar condition including this condition being imposed upon the subsequent purchaser.

To sisterhood

Contents

'Seriousness, like life, is a thought and this thought creates a feeling. And if you create the feeling of seriousness then you are in a very serious state. You are very liable to have stress and strain and sickness and unhappiness and jealousy and everything else because of seriousness. Now seriousness doesn't help you do anything in life but destroy yourself.'

– **Sydney Banks** (audio, no date)

Introduction

At a time when the world seems to be in turmoil with environmental and other issues causing us to question many aspects of our lives and the way we live, it's easy to take life very seriously. After all, why wouldn't we take life seriously?!

The idea for this book struck at three o'clock in the morning in July 2020 in the midst of the first Covid lockdown in the UK.

At that time, I was reluctantly home-schooling my kids, furloughed from my job as a project manager at a national charity and volunteering for another organisation (just in case I didn't have a job to go back to). My husband's work situation was also in flux and I observed myself going in and out of 'serious thinking' about our 'situation', home-schooling and the state of the world.

I saw that when I was in my head resisting what is, I wasn't present to the wonder of my children and the beauty of the nature around me. I also saw that I was resisting and putting a lid on the essence and source of creativity and possibility that was bubbling under the surface, ready to burst forth when I let my personal thinking get out of the way and was able to just be.

Then in the middle of the night inspiration struck and I felt compelled to write the vision for this book.

What had led to that flash of inspiration was an eleven-year transformative journey of seeing and understanding how my experience of life is created, which has enabled me to reconnect to my essence beyond the chatter of my thinking. During this time, I have met and been taught by some incredible people, some of whom feature in this book. (You can read more about this understanding in the 'Note to the Reader', page 7.)

There were also other influences that contributed to this idea and my feeling to write a book primarily aimed at women, which came as a surprise, even to me!

In the months leading up to that moment I had been hosting women's wellbeing sessions for Nisa-Nashim, the Jewish–Muslim women's network I am part of, which had reinforced in me the power in having women-only spaces for reflection.

I had also read several books that had left a big impression on me:

- Reading *Climate Justice: A Man-Made Problem with A Feminist Solution* by Mary Robinson (2019), I was struck by the power in amplifying women's unheard voices.
- *Invisible Women* by Caroline Criado Perez (2020) showed me the stark reality of how research is not designed in ways that enable women to have their voices heard and the detrimental impact this has not only on women themselves but also on society as a whole.
- Toni Packer's (2007) *The Light of Discovery* showed me once again how much I had been living in my head and helped me to see even more, the beauty of living life in the moment.

Then in April 2020 I had the opportunity to hear a talk by an inspiring African American woman whose teenage son had been mistakenly stopped by the police on the way to school and handcuffed for 30 minutes while they were on the lookout for a suspect in the local area. It had really affected him in ways she was concerned would impact how he would react in the future if something like this happened again. She was very upset by this because she could see that what happened had taken something away from her son's value as a person, so he felt that he was now the typical young, Black, male statistic. But instead of staying bothered by this, she went beyond her serious thinking and she was able to interpret what had happened as an 'unfortunate innocent situation'. She phoned up the local police station and reached out to them. She explained to the police what had happened and told them she needed them to come round to her house to talk to her son – as she didn't want it to be that next time he came in contact with them he would act out of fear without clear judgement because he felt like he was being attacked or they were messing with him. So the police came round and together they were able to defuse the situation. Her son was better able to understand that it was the system and not personal.

That story had a big impact on me because I saw in it the power in going beyond our serious thinking and what impact that could have in the world. If that mother could be in touch with her wisdom in such difficult circumstances and do that, what would be possible in the world if more of us were able to see fresh ways of dealing powerfully with life from a place of wisdom and insight rather than a place of fear and habitual thinking?

It occurred to me that it would be inspiring for people to hear from a diverse group of women who have seen the power in looking in the opposite direction to their serious thinking and the impact that has had on them and their lives. And perhaps through reading these personal stories the people who read the book may get to see beyond their serious, self-limiting thinking so that their own light shines brighter in the world.

The seed was planted, but I had to wait a few months to water it before I could have the capacity to start speaking to people and let it grow, and even longer before I could start to see it come to fruition.

During that time George Floyd was ruthlessly murdered, climate change continues to wreak even more havoc in the world and many of us are finding our lives to be in a constant state of flux, more than they ever were before. This has caused many of us (myself included) to question many aspects of our lives and the way we live them. Often these issues go beyond our personal circumstances – which for each of us in our own ways may be challenging in their own right – so there is a lot we can be serious about.

I had many beautiful conversations that led to the personal stories you will read about in this book from ordinary and inspiring women like you and me who have seen beyond their serious thinking in many different aspects of their lives.

Some share how they were able to go beyond their inner demons, such as Susan Marmot whose lack of self-worth impacted her relationships, Jenny Elleray who had a life-long struggle with her self-image, and Lucy Sheffield and Jan Armstrong who struggled with addiction.

Some relate to how they dealt with what any of us would perceive as challenging personal circumstances in unexpected and refreshing ways: Elaine Hilides who shares her often humorous outlook on her breast cancer diagnosis, and Debra Simmons who shares how she was able to be there for her son in the most difficult of circumstances.

Others talk about their experiences of seeing beyond their serious thinking in day-to-day life, such as Farah Halabi who gave up on trying to be the best mum in the world, Sarah McAreavey whose holiday disaster helped her learn some useful life lessons, and Jacquie Forde who was able to get beyond her fearful thinking at a business meeting.

Others like Ami Chen Mills-Naim, Julieanne Chazotte and Karen Evanoff share their insights into how they and we can face up to this century's ultimate challenges without having the weight of the world on our shoulders.

Many have been on the ultimate quest for answers in their lives only to find them closer to home than they ever imagined.

When I read these stories I can relate to every single one of them as they speak to the core of my being, even though I haven't been through the same experiences.

On the surface, all the women featured in this book come from different backgrounds, countries, cultures, religions, etc., but beneath what we and others may define ourselves to be, at our essence we are all one. Just as humanity is one.

Who am I, who are any of us but the stories we tell ourselves and others? When we see beyond these stories, what then becomes possible for us and for the world?

I invite you to reflect on these questions as you read this book in whatever way makes sense to you, either from cover to cover or dipping in and out reflecting on the stories and experiences that speak to you.

Much love

George Halfin

October 2021

Note to the Reader

All the women who have contributed to this book come from a place of understanding of how their experience of life is created via the gift of thought. Seeing this simple yet profound understanding has enabled them to gain perspective on their lives and, in some cases, to unlearn habits of a lifetime that have held them back from being a true expression of who they are in the world.

This understanding points to the formless side of life which is before and beyond words, practices and actions. It is something innate to all of us regardless of our culture, religious affiliation, country of birth, sexuality or gender. So deep down it is something all of us know to be true – it may have just become hidden over the course of our lifetime.

You will find what people are pointing to in this book in many spiritual teachings and even in some scientific ones. For all of us who have contributed to this book, we have come to this understanding via the teachings of a man called Sydney Banks who was a Scottish welder living and working on Salt Spring Island off the coast of Vancouver, Canada, in the 1970s who had an enlightenment experience which led to him sharing his profound insights into the human experience. Since then, many people around the world have shared this understanding under a number of names including *The Three Principles, Innate Health, The Inside Out understanding, Clarity,* and *Health Realization*. Thousands of people including those in this book have been impacted by this under-standing which is now taught in many different places, includ-ing schools, prisons, homeless shelters, businesses and troubled council estates/housing projects.

There are many books, videos and articles available which explain what The Three Principles are in simple terms – and you can easily look this up on the internet and find an explanation that speaks to you. For the purposes of this book, I have decided not to attempt to do this as to me the stories are an expression of this understanding which speak to the heart of it, and any kind of explanation may get in the way of you truly hearing what is conveyed in these stories by trying to intellectually under-stand the explanation given. That was certainly my experience when I stumbled across this understanding over eleven years ago – so I invite you to submerge yourself in these stories and be open to what comes up for you when you read them. Then if you are curious to know more you can explore for yourself the wealth of resources that are available. You can also find supple-mentary videos from contributors and additional resources at **alifelessserious.club**

A Life Less Serious, a poem

Elizabeth Lovius

This living life to plan
What we should do, who we must be
Achieving all we can.

We carry a hefty burden
Of what we need to be
A heavy load, that weighs us down
And stops us running free.

We also have a wilder side
Where nature shows the way
Where we can laugh and lighten up
The sweet, wild path of play.

I hear you cry, 'that's nice for some'
Responsibilities
Are what my life is made up of
How can I just be me?

A mother's lot is guilt assured
It just comes with the job
So much to do, so little time
The hearth, the home, the hob.

And raising kids is super-tough
They are so innocent
At any moment life goes wrong
We must be vigilant.

We have to balance life AND work
Which takes another toll
To knuckle down and get results
We must stay in control.

So yes it looks quite serious
To have to juggle balls
And dropping them is not ideal
Someone might see our flaws.

But what if we had missed the point
Of what life's all about?
Enjoyment is our one true path
To follow without doubt.

When we are fully living free
From blood and soul and heart
We feel the Spirit move through us
And 'shoulds' start to depart.

For each of us is blessed to have
A wise and inner guide
That soft, clear simple wisdom
That speaks from deep inside.

It speaks of what is good for us
What will improve this day
It speaks of lightness and of love
It points us out the way.

To then become our pure, bright light
Each road mysterious
For each of us was born to live;
A life less serious.

My Story is Pretty Ordinary

Linda Ramus

Greetings Fellow Pilgrims, my story is pretty ordinary. No head-peeling 'aha' OMG insight. More simply like a continuous series of 'yeah that makes sense' moments. It's been like just a drip, drip, drip of water on stone because that's what my head was (is), a block of rock-hard intellect. So for me, learning about the understanding of The Three Principles (see the 'Note to the Reader', page 7) has been a journey from my life as a government management analyst not navigating my inner life very well and taking life way too seriously to taking things less seriously and living in more contentment than I could have ever imagined.

But really, talk about being hard-headed, it took a 2,108-mile walk in the woods to loosen me up enough to hear something about The Three Principles. In 1995, my husband and I decided to hike the Appalachian Trail, Georgia to Maine. Never did really determine whose brilliant idea that was. So for six months there I was just walking every day up and down a pretty punishing trail that rendered me almost nonverbal and effectively shut down my analyst's brain, setting me up to hear something that would change my life.

By all the usual measures, I was doing alright in life, doing the right things, college education, good job, wonderful husband, financially secure, good health. However, I can't say I was really happy or felt much contentment and peace of mind. I still had anger issues, let the job get to me, cursed at traffic... (still do sometimes because that is still a stage of enlightenment I have not yet attained). But in 1995 one of us had the brilliant idea to go hike the Appalachian Trail—'the road less traveled'—and really, 'that has made all the difference.' So there I was, on April 1, 1995, standing on top of Springer Mountain, Georgia looking north to Maine suddenly feeling overwhelmed with the thought of walking 2,108 miles. How do you do that? Then I heard a voice inside say 'One step and then another step and then another.' So that became my trail name, 'One Step.'

Today I know that simply was my inner wisdom just giving me the simple answer. Nothing complicated, just simple truth, 'take one step, then another.' It really is pretty much all you need to navigate life. I have also come to know and experience that it will also tell me what type of step to take. In this case it was actual footsteps. So all I need to do is ask and listen.

Over the next six months I realized the 'step' very much also included a mental as well as physical aspect. As one famous thru-hiker Grandma Gatewood said, 'It takes more head than heel.' The more I have learned about The Three Principles, the more I understand the truth of that and that each step is just the next thought that propels me down the trail, that pushes me through the hard parts and brings me the joy and the beauty of the trail. 'One thought and then another, and another.' My trail name probably should have been One Thought but I think that is already taken. However, this long walk I came to see was the prerequisite for me being able to have an insight about what The Three Principles said about the true nature of experience.

So when I returned to work, unable to put two thoughts together, unable to really crank up the ol' analyst brain to its pre-hike levels. My friend Cathy Casey invited me to this workshop with this guy Dr Roger Mills. She was one of his presenters at this workshop. While I was on the trail I knew she had gotten into this 'weird' stuff, something about The Three Principles. I knew I had to check it out to make sure she hadn't gotten into some California 'new-age-y' cult thing. My boss told me to go as I was still pretty useless at my job.

Not a head-peeler like I said, but what I heard deeply was that every human being has wisdom and common sense. No exceptions. What I heard satisfied my still analytical self that 'yeah, this makes sense.' What I experienced was just enough insight to know I wanted to learn more. So that is what I have been doing for the past twenty-five years as both teacher and student. I admit, I am a slow learner.

You see, what I heard at this initial workshop was that we all have within us, at the core of our being, this spiritual wisdom, common sense—call it whatever you like—that has been and is always there. A big part of my journey since then has been to become better at listening to and trusting that inner voice. The answer is always there. It is so practical that it has helped me repair a car. It is also so wise and loving that it guided me, comforted me and took care of me when my husband died on a backpacking trip in Oregon in 2003. It is our operator's handbook, our instruction manual for life—but how many people attempt to put the treadmill together without first reading the instructions? How many times do we have to be told, 'when all else fails, read the instructions'?

For the past twenty-five years I have been both a student and a teacher. I have taught what I understand of the Principles in jails, prison, treatment programs, homeless shelters, domestic abuse programs and to hundreds of human services professionals. While often feeling inadequate to the job, I know to just teach what I know and that the more I share the more I get back.

The trail, however, continues to be a place where theory gets real. The trail is often hard, sometimes life-threatening, but always life-affirming. It is having to live in the unknown without a lot of control over what happens next. So it was in 2019 while on a 700-mile hike of the Pacific Crest Trail in the desert of southern California on a day just like any other trail day, on a steep climb on a hot afternoon like a lot of other hot steep climbs, for whatever unknown reason, I 'got it,' acceptance. Not a head-peeler but I felt it, just a quiet feeling. The trail just is what it is. It's not personal. No matter how hot or steep the trail is, it just is. With that insight I quit struggling and just took that next step. Life too is just what it is. There is a thru-hiker saying, 'embrace the suck.' Yeah, I really love thru-hiker no-frills wisdom.

I know it may not seem like a big deal but like I said, I'm pretty ordinary and it's these quiet little 'hits' that have added up over the years and one day I noticed things are different.

Here is another piece of thru-hiker wisdom, 'Hike your own hike.'

Happy Trails,

One Step.

My Bumpy, Lumpy and Beautiful Human Experience

Bronwen Warner

When I hit thirty-nine, I started to panic. I panicked because I knew that I was nowhere near having my shit together by the time I turned forty. I thought I'd be thin. I thought I'd be rich. I thought I'd know for sure what my purpose was at least! Of course, once these three things were in place, I believed I'd be happy, content, changing the world for the better, and no longer a stressed-out, shouting mother.

When I was thirty-four, my brother who was two years younger than me, was murdered. Two months before he died, I lost my dad and, just six weeks after, I gave birth to my second daughter. My oldest daughter was two years old at the time. I didn't know how to cope. I didn't know how to feel the pain. I didn't know how things could ever be OK again.

Grief shows up in many ways. For me, what I see now, was that in an effort to distract myself from the pain and the gaping hole in my soul, I got busy. (I also ate cake but that's another story.)

I decided that my life had to mean something. That there had to be a purpose both for my life and for my brother's life. His death had to mean something. It seemed real to me that I now had to live life for both of us and I had better live it to the max. I started and stopped a lot of projects. I fundraised, I blogged, I took on crazy challenges like One Hundred Burpees for One Hundred Days, I mothered, I worked, I quit my job, I found new work, I started businesses.

I would lie awake at 3 a.m. every night for years on end, my mind overflowing with ideas, possible products and creative content to try. I bought domain names by the dozen and spent hours tinkering on websites. I discovered and diagnosed myself with new conditions:

- Impostor syndrome (fear of being found out for not knowing what you're doing).
- Shiny object syndrome (fear of committing to one thing and always getting distracted by the next shiny new thing).
- Comparisonitis (fear of never being as good as someone else, often resulting in fear of being seen).
- FOMO (fear of missing out – missing out on what I'm not sure but it meant I got distracted a lot).

These were alongside the labels of PTSD, depression, anxiety, compulsive binge eating, and extreme rage at everything and everyone. All these together added up to me believing, and friends, family and professionals agreeing, that I was broken and needed fixing.

So, I set off on a quest. I found myself obsessed with searching for answers. I spent thousands of pounds and countless hours listening to other people's breakthroughs, solutions and insights.

I devoured course after book after webinar, convinced that, this time, what the 'expert' taught would be enough for me to get inspired enough to 'do the work', make the money I needed and fulfil my purpose, whatever that was supposed to be.

I went to therapy for answers. I couldn't understand what was wrong with me. I couldn't get my act together. I couldn't do what I thought I needed to do. I found myself feeling worse and worse and worse. All my days were laced with fear.

'Where do you think fear comes from?' my friend asked.

We were sitting on blue chairs facing each other. There were no windows in the room, so it was lit up by square light panels in the ceiling, even though the sun outside was shining. The training room was efficient yet cosy with yellow cushion-covered step seating at the back and heavy blue curtains breaking up the monotonous expanse of the walls. I was hot in my light blue cardigan, a slight coating of sweat at the back of my neck where my long hair smothered it. The smell of someone's takeaway coffee was strong in the air. A balled-up tissue was on the floor by my friend's foot. There were nineteen other course participants having conversations between themselves so the buzz in the room was loud but, for me, my awareness of it had shrunk. All my senses were directed inwards. My mind went quiet as the question lasered through the never-ending chatter that, until that moment, I had not realised was so incessant. With the crystal clearness that comes with fresh thought or insight, I noticed with surprise the answer that came to me.

'It's coming from me,' I said.

My mind was officially blown! All that time believing that my circumstances were causing me to be afraid and fearful. All that time spent looking outside of myself for answers. All that time I had it wrong! In that moment I saw that it was me who was causing me to be afraid. I saw that there were some thoughts that I was paying way too much attention to that were causing all my suffering. I saw that I didn't have to do that anymore.

Even more than that, I saw that all that time spent in fear and stress, worrying, planning and trying to figure out what to do next was such a waste of energy. I saw that all along, things had been happening without me having to be involved. I saw that something had my back. When I was in the depths of grief and depression, with two small babies, something in me helped me to do what needed to be done to keep them fed, well and loved. When I needed to make money, something helped me to know what to do and how to get the next bit of income. When I was eating copious amounts of cake for years on end, there was something helping me to cope in the best way I could at the time.

Life had been unfolding, in spite of me.

After that bombshell of an insight, I'd love to say that I became a fearless warrior who took on the world and made all my dreams come true.

Not quite.

Here's what did happen:

I stopped expecting answers from other people's experiences and opinions.

I was so fixated on other people's words about the path that had worked for them that I couldn't see - couldn't trust - my own path. The way I do life, business, parenting, can only be unique to me, the same way my response to grief was. Like snowflakes.

Each is different yet perfect. I have way fewer expectations of myself and others now.

I got so much more creative.

I started to play with creativity. I noticed that I was already creating so much in my life every day that the story I had about myself being uncreative just didn't seem like it could be true anymore. Every day, dinner was being made, despite not having a clue what to do half an hour before. Every day, I responded to the challenges my kids threw at me. Every day I entertained, broke up fights, found things to do on long, rainy lockdown days. I started writing and noticed how pages got filled even though I never knew where to start. There were formless ideas and then, often as if by magic, there it was, in form. That is creativity and we cannot separate ourselves from it. I stopped looking outside of myself for inspiration and trusted my own ideas much more.

With so much gratitude, the whole concept of purpose has changed for me. I live, that is my purpose. That I live is magical, phenomenal and quite how I exist at all in this intricate, breathing, cell-dividing, blood-pumping body is beyond my limited ability to understand. The fact that I live, and that there is a power that's driving me that has nothing to do with me, has made me so much more grateful for all of my bumpy, lumpy and beautiful human experience.

I'm less serious about work.

I'm less serious about fear.

I'm less serious about myself.

I'm less serious about life.

The Old Cashmere Shawl

Liliana Bellini

It's early morning and I'm sitting at the dining table looking outside. My mid-March garden is being showered by rain. The house is silent so I have a chance to sit back and take in the sound of the rain.

I take it in without any resistance, it has to be one of my favourite sounds. Soothing to my soul, washing over me and the garden. As I am being awakened by it, I let out a sigh of relief.

I welcome these quiet moments like a caress, unexpected and unplanned.

I welcome the soft feeling that comes over me, through me, from within me.

I welcome how it wraps around me and invites me back to the here and now. It feels like that old cashmere shawl my mother left behind after she passed.

There is nothing softer than that shawl.

So I let go, how can I not? I let the feeling caress me, the shawl embrace me. I let this moment hold me, and for a while which feels like forever, this moment holds me.

Then, I find myself gliding through time, through months and years until I'm back in my mother's bedroom; it must have been the memory of the shawl. It was a month before she died and we had not realised how quickly it would happen. Within three months of the diagnosis she was gone.

In the twenty-five years since I left Italy, I had visited countless times. At first with friends, then with a husband, with babies in slings, toddlers under my feet and later with grumpy teenagers, many Christmases, summer holidays, half-terms.

This time I was there on my own, just to be with mum and dad. I wanted to help and I wondered if this time she would let me.

I found her in bed, in her white cotton nightie.

'Ciao mamma, I'm here,' I said.

It was a strange sight as I had never seen her in bed, at midday, in her white cotton nightie. The wooden shutters were ajar, softening the midday light of that sunny winter day. Her bedroom looked like it had always done, tidy, with its oak furniture which was sober and designed to last.

The old cashmere shawl was resting on top of the linen trunk at the foot of the bed, folded.

On the dressing table next to her bed, six small pictures in silver frames were lined up like little soldiers. They were baby pictures of her grandsons in chronological order. Next to them there was the small bottle of holy water she had brought back some years before from her pilgrimage in Lourdes. On the pillow next to her there was a small rosary, the short 'condensed' one with fewer beads, the one she used to carry in her handbag inside its silk pouch.

I could see she looked different. Her short silver hair hadn't been trimmed for a while and she had lost some weight, but her robust frame had not yet given in to the illness. Her face was flushed and there was a glow to her skin that I wasn't expecting. She was looking at me smiling, and in her eyes I could see a light I hadn't seen in many years.

For some reason, it reminded me of how her face looked during the summer months, up in the mountains in our little house.

It was where she was at her happiest. It was what she called 'La Mia Casa', 'My Home'.

I stood there, in the doorway of her bedroom and took her in. I stood there and hesitated, as I had never been allowed in her bedroom, it was off-limits to my sister and me. We had never been allowed to sit or lie on her bed either. She had always made her bed with the finest linen and in that special way she had learned when she was a nurse, before she married my dad. It was immaculate. Nobody could make a bed like mum did. My sister eventually learned but I never did.

As a young girl I would sometimes sneak in and explore this part of the house that was foreign to me. I would open her drawers, her wardrobe, her boxes, secretly hoping to find signs of a different kind of mother. A mother who read gossip magazines, who wore make up, high heels, and that perfume I smelled on some of the other mothers.

There was never any sign of that kind of woman. Her wardrobe smelled of lavender and her clothes, most of which she made herself, hung in silence and in perfect order. There was never any dust and everything had its place.

My mamma, this stoic woman who lived her own version of a monastic life, wearing her apron every day like a religious robe. With rigidity and dignity. With pain and resentment. With 'a hard something' that I later discovered was a form of love.

She always stood strong, firmly planted to the ground, with her broad shoulders and her straight posture, proud. She had been majestic and intimidating; it was her my boyfriends feared, not my dad. Often she had been intolerant of us, of me, of any kind of frivolity, of noise, of life.

So, on that day, a month before she died when I found her in bed at midday, I asked myself 'why the glow on her face and the spark in her eyes?'

'Come here love, and sit on my bed,' she said.

I did as I was told and sat on her bed next to her.

I let myself be taken into her arms, and over the next ten days, I let myself be led into this other world neither of us ever thought we would visit together. A different world just behind the heavy cloth that had covered her life.

In those days, I saw that cloth fall down onto the carpeted floor of her bedroom and disappear, for good. It carried the weight of a story she had been telling herself for most of her life, words written with a permanent marker all over it. A collection of rules and conditions, of dos and don'ts and religious dogmas. A story of silent insults and blame towards people from her past, towards herself and towards life itself.

The mother behind the cloth was a person I didn't know, but who somehow felt more familiar than the one who raised me. I smiled as I wondered, 'what were you doing mamma, hiding behind that cloth all your life?'

I took a deep breath as I realised that the part of her which was allowed to be experienced during the last few months of her life had been there all along.

She was the one whose face glowed and whose eyes sparkled.

So we prayed and laughed and cried and we talked, but not too much, and then we prayed a bit more.

And I noticed that mum was no longer holding on to the rosary as if her sanity and her life depended on it. Instead, she had a light touch with it, in how she held it and in the way she recited it, almost as if she was singing a nursery rhyme instead of asking for deliverance.

When she grew too tired to pray, speak or eat, she slept a lot. I lay next to her and took in her presence, deep within me, in a room and on a bed that were no longer off-limits.

I held her hand and I memorised the liver spots on the skin, a whole constellation of them.

I remember being aware of a thought going through my mind, like a wooden stick being carried by the gentle current of a river. The thought said something like – 'why now mamma, why did it take you so long to wake up to this?' – but the thought floated away just as easily as it had come and I was left with her in that moment which was complete and perfect as it was.

After those ten days with mum I had to come back to London to assist a lady through the birth of her first child. She was a single lady, a client I had been supporting through pregnancy and who I had also committed to support through childbirth.

The labour had been long and difficult and ended with the birth of a little girl. Due to some complications in the final stage of the delivery, the mother had to be taken to theatre to have postnatal surgery.

I had been at many births and held many babies, including my own. They had all been different, all miracles I had the privilege of witnessing.

However, this was the first time that nobody was there to hold the baby, only me.

'Can I leave her with you for a while?' the midwife asked.

I was sitting on a hospital chair, in a busy labour ward, in the early hours of a clear, crisp winter morning, sleep-deprived. I had been awake for twenty-four hours; the sunlight crashing through the large window felt too sharp for my sore eyes. I needed a hot shower and my teeth brushed but in that moment nothing felt more perfect than spending time with her, just the two of us.

'Of course,' I said.

The midwife placed the baby in my arms. I received this tiny, pristine, new human being like a gift, a jewel wrapped in a blanket. We looked at each other for a long time, with intent and curiosity. She saw me, and she knew me.

Had we met before?

I fell into the deep blue inside her eyes. It was a bottomless well of silence and wonders, of pure potential and presence, of inherent knowing.

She was old and wise, she was young and free.

She was my daughter, she was my sister and my best friend.

She was my mother when we were up in the mountains in summer, in the little house she called her home.

She was the light I saw in my mother's eyes the month before she died.

Identity, Earth and Flowers

Karen Evanoff

In early spring when the grip of winter was loosening, it was the musty smell of earth and the tiny yellow buttercup flowers that informed me of seasons changing. As a little girl, I always wanted to get closer to these first signs of the earth waking up, this ignited something inside me. I would sit behind our two-room log cabin, leaning against the graying logs with a stick in hand and poke into the thawing mud. The smell became stronger when I did this. Buttercups grew on clumps of grass along the beach and I would bend low on my knees to look at every detail of the small flowers that had many bluish lines along each petal, and in the center was a sponge-like softness that drew my curious hands in.

I was safe in the comfort of simple village life in remote Alaska. Fewer than two hundred people with no road connection to the outside world. In many ways we lived similar to the way our ancestors did. The biggest change was being sedentary versus nomadic, due to the requirement for children to receive an education at a stationary school. We still harvested food from the land and lived outside most of the time. My dad had a dog team for transportation, we bathed in hot steam baths (like saunas), and carried water and wood into the house. I saw lots of laughter, back then, teasing and joking. My dad would sit and talk in our language with other adults, they would laugh and laugh, exchanging stories. I didn't understand what they were saying but I felt their aliveness and their joy.

When more changes to our way of life happened, I was not prepared for how these changes impacted the adults in the community. The energy shifted from simple and light to serious and overly responsible. When I look back today, I could see how the sense of powerlessness took over. I saw my dad suddenly become angry at outsiders. Some of the outsiders and changes included: law enforcers managing our harvests of fish and game; a village corporation being created under the Alaska Native Claims Settlement Act 1971 (ANCSA) and land ownership and making money becoming a road map; and local tribal and city governments run by state and federal laws which didn't align with our community values. My dad rarely laughed, joked, or spoke our language anymore; he stood up in public meetings, voicing his concerns. Fighting for land protection and being able to hunt based on traditional laws became his main activities. My mom was driven by the need to fit in; as she was part white with light skin, she was targeted as being different in the community—she coped by keeping to herself and cried easily. Her strength came through in our family as a solid stable presence; she kept a clean home and food on the table.

The adjustments to our community changed my parents and what they stood for. I didn't see these patterned changes until I was older.

The smell of sweet earth and the sight of buttercup flowers faded to the background. As a young adult, I began to understand what all the unsettledness was about and this moved me to work toward positive change. What a journey that has been, as I stepped into the footsteps of anger at systems and the authority governed by another culture. I became righteous and frustrated. Flight or fight drove me. Working for change was a serious business and I held a lot of responsibility. I worked hard to sober up an (ex) husband and I worked hard to change systems.

Now the current system I work for is under the federal government and I have been here for close to twenty years. I took this job mostly because the mission is about land protection and preservation of cultures. My job is to document, to preserve cultural knowledge and the revitalization of certain skill sets, and traditional knowledge is part of this work. I wasn't fully aware at the time I took the job of what drew me to this work.

Connection. Heart connection. Something beyond my storied mind and the memories that drove me.

The wisdom of the cultural knowledge I worked to document gave me a feeling of aliveness. There was something in what I heard that ignited the same feeling I had as a little girl smelling thawing earth and leaning close to yellow flowers. I always felt something else present beyond the world around me. But keeping busy and the need for change got more of my attention.

Outside of the wisdom and spirituality I learned from my own culture and other indigenous groups, I spent many years seeking other spiritual practices and teachers. This seeking began in 1989 when I was working as a counselor in the village and I started training for this position. I learned about codependency first. Then the effects of alcoholism on families and Al-Anon.* My training was to gain tools to support my position as a counselor. I saw clearly that I was as much of a candidate as the people I was counseling. I did a lot of 'work' to change those patterns and habits over the years. Bottom line was that it was work! To think positive and have compassion and not react and not enable and sit still and meditate for hours, and the list goes on, is work. And then I heard a recording by Syd Banks that my Al-Anon sponsor at the time had emailed me. 'You might get something out of this...' she wrote.

The main thing I heard from this talk was 'You are already whole and complete, you can stop your searching.' What a concept! I had studied and practiced various methods that point to spirituality and wellbeing for years and not once had I heard this. Those words gave me permission and a deeper awareness of the subtle 'something beyond' that I always felt. And the thought thing. I didn't realize how much power I gave my thoughts. I learned that this was not about making my thoughts go away but noticing my feelings directly pointed to what I am thinking. I have a choice, if I am feeling unsettled or in a bad mood or even anxious, this is a big one for me, I can see my thoughts for what they are and move on or stay with each thought and continue feeling like shit! Simple!

I have experienced many positive changes with the realization of my wholeness. I feel the ever-present energy of a humble loving power behind the life around me. I've seen my own story as an

---

Al-Anon are support groups for friends and families of alcoholics.

Indigenous or Native American person and how much that story has limited me. I also see how certain patterns of these stories became themes throughout entire cultures. Not just Indigenous but what we call the western or mainstream culture. As a child the earth spoke to me and kept my spirit alive. The deep relationship between humans and earth is what is most important to me. That is my passion. What we care about, we will care for. We need to remember that we were all Indigenous at one time. We all have ancestors who ate from the land, sat around fires telling stories, had ceremonies and rituals and humor that supported the spirit. We all had ancestors who took care of and maintained the land in its original form, never depleting an area, never taking more than is needed. As I have documented and recorded Elders telling these ancestral stories, this has become even more important to me. We all need to remember what worked in keeping our earth intact was the human relationship revolving around the deep spiritual connection in all its beauty and humble offerings. This is not a remembering of the intellect. It is a remembering of the heart.

The culture I come from, as many others, has experienced dramatic changes. I was never a victim of these changes but for many years I believed I was so I was driven by anger. I was angry, defensive, and righteously opinionated at the white culture whose influences and forced systems seemed to dominate our way of life. Now, I know, they too live by made-up rules of patterned habits. My waking up has realigned my true power to a source so much bigger than me. Culture and tradition are continually being re-created by the people who live them.

Today, I strive to re-create first as an individual human being.

Today, through a conscious connection to the intelligence of the heart, I feel the same aliveness I did as a child.

Today, as I hear each patterned story that was passed on to me and those I made up to cope, I envision the healing of those before me.

My parents, grandparents, and ancestors.

Today I feel hope for the future and joy in potential and evolving possibilities.

And the good news is, I don't need to work so hard for any of this!

The Upside of Struggle – Waking up from Within Again and Again

Jenny Elleray

One of my earliest memories is sitting at the dinner table with my mum, dad and sister. I would have been about two and a half years old. I said something funny, and everyone laughed. I burst into tears and hid under the table. This is just one of countless memories of crying when people laughed at me, looked at me the wrong way or asked me a question I didn't know the answer to. It became a common theme throughout my childhood, teens and early twenties.

I can see now so clearly that at a young age I had become very serious about myself, extremely self-conscious, and completely paranoid that people were in some way being unkind to me, laughing at me, judging me.

I was described as shy; I found eye contact with people very difficult, especially adults. My sister luckily used to step in and excuse me, 'Jenny's just shy'. She would answer questions for me too. I lived in so much embarrassment, anxiety and fear of being put in a situation where I would feel uncomfortable.

I think going to primary school forced me to be a little braver, I had good friends and nice teachers. I also had my big sister there to sort things out for me. I remember the sadness and fear I felt when she left for secondary school.

I had an inability to laugh at myself, I was so easily upset or offended, and I ended up making life very small. At thirteen, my self-consciousness became focused mainly on my looks. I was obsessed with every perceived imperfection, completely paranoid that I was ugly, my teeth were wonky, my hair was the wrong colour, my legs were too short. I hated my freckles, my hands were too big, my fingers weren't straight enough, I was too fat. I turned myself into a monster in the mirror.

This soon turned to anorexia and bulimia, and with these came even more self-loathing. I then turned to drugs and binge drinking to be able to cope with the social aspects of being a teenager. My poor little growing body, I put it through so much.

I look back now and can see that I had become chronically self-obsessed. I took myself so seriously, I believed all the negative thoughts that ran through my head. I was terrified of my feelings and did anything I could to try to avoid feeling them.

At twenty-three years old my sister invited me on a course with Dr Roger Mills and Margaret Opio in London. Over the three days, my mind became quiet and my attention shifted from self-focus and criticism to deep listening. I felt like a space had been revealed within me that was at the same time familiar but also completely unknown. It was like I saw my character start to crumble and fall away. All of the ideas of me were suddenly just that, ideas, thoughts, beliefs, but from this new space it all felt so distant, so intangible.

I left with a sense of peace, calm and infinite possibility. I could see that, by taking myself so seriously my whole life, it had seemed to me that life really was serious. My problems, my looks, my weight, my mood, all of it had consumed my being. It was as if Roger and Margaret just pointed out to me that who I thought I was, was not true or fixed. It was a bunch of ideas and beliefs that together made up a character who struggled their way through life.

I realised that there was really only one thing permanent about me, and that was the awareness of my life. I saw that I had changed uncountable times throughout my life, likes and dislikes, I had learnt, grown and believed. I could see the innocence and misunderstanding that I had lived in. I had identified with a load of made-up concepts, rather than the unknowable creative force that allowed me to dream my life into being. No wonder life had seemed so hard.

It's hard to find the words to describe what happened that sunny May of 2005. I've heard people say I had a shift in consciousness or an insight. I honestly do not know. I would love to be able to put it into words or a formula for someone else to see, but I know that what took place within me was beyond words, beyond this world. The beautiful thing is that now I can only see wholeness, in myself and in others. I can see the fleeting moods and emotions for what they are – thoughts bringing to life our experience in each moment, but the moment is forever resigned to memory the instant we are in a new moment.

I feel that humanity has lived in the dark ages of the mind for so long, so many have forgotten their true nature, lost in a world of thoughts and concepts, unwittingly creating hell on earth for themselves. There have been great teachers and guides throughout time quietly whispering a remembering to us, and those who heard have woken from the nightmare of their own minds to the beauty that exists at the heart of life and have then gone on to share with others.

So, it is difficult to say that I myself turned away from seriousness, as it seems to me that seriousness never really was. I didn't have to work at seeing it anew, it was done through me. So much of what I have now come to see, I had heard someone else say, or read in a book, but until I saw it for myself it meant nothing, and had no impact on my life. I always remember my mum giving me a book about 'Feeling the fear, and doing it anyway' as a teenager, but it seemed so far away, just someone else's good ideas. I couldn't work out a way to implement them in my life. In a funny way the more people tried to help me, the more I would feel like a failure when I then didn't change. I used to go to bed listening to a hypnosis tape – 'Supreme self-confidence' – and each morning I woke, feeling no better than the night before. I was looking for someone to fix me. Then in 2005 I realised I couldn't be fixed, as I was never broken.

I have gone on to share as best I can with people around the world what I have come to realise about life. I have been present to see so many others wake up from within themselves to their true nature and go on to live beautiful lives navigating the inevitable ups and downs with so much grace and wisdom.

My life since May 2005 has been an incredible ride! I have travelled the world filming and sharing what is known as The Three Principles, or Innate Health. I have been married, divorced, lost loved ones, changed careers, moved numerous times. I have experienced joy, love, hope, peace, sorrow, frustration, pain. I have felt more deeply than ever before the contrasts in experience. I have created whole new personas and then watched them crumble again before my eyes. It appears who we are is a moving target, no sooner than you think you have it pinned down, it's moved, changed, transformed, but waking up to see the illusion of the movement and target changed everything.

The last six years with my husband Dave especially have been ones of shedding layers of unseen thoughts, and aspects of myself. What I hadn't realised is how easy it is to buy in to your own creation and think, right this is it, this is the true me! I had replaced my eating disorder with healthy clean living, which sounds great, but then that soon became its own kind of mental prison. Needing to exercise and eat a certain way, still very focused on the body, and to be honest still incredibly vain. As those layers have been shed, I have seen how easy it actually is to live a healthy life. It never needed the amount of energy I gave it, the wisdom and intelligence are there if we just listen. I now enjoy life too much to be so vain! I am boring to myself; I am far more interested now in the beautiful world that I live in. I can get lost in listening to the birds, sit in a kayak completely transfixed by the way the light falls on the ripples in the water, swim in freezing lakes and tarns, sit in awe at the way the trees gently move in the wind. Sunsets, rain drops, trees, ants, spiders, Rusty our Jack Russell – all reminders of the remarkable nature of nature. And we are nature.

We are infinitely creative beings, and if our focus falls away from ourselves, and into the moment, we start to create far more joy in our lives – I wish that for everyone on Earth.

Finding Flow in Relationships

Susan Marmot

If you have looked for a loving relationship that really works for as long as I did then it will be no surprise to hear it felt like a very serious business. I feared I may go through the whole of my life without having the experience of love I longed for and hoped for.

Whether in a relationship or single I would think a lot. When I was single I would have self-doubt and lack of self-worth. It felt painful and hard. My mind would run away and paranoia would set in and I would spiral down into thinking about how others perceived me. Do they like me? Did I do something wrong? I felt unprotected and exposed. Depending on the day, going out could feel like an unknown and scary proposition as I had no idea what people might say to me or how resilient I would feel. I could end up feeling exposed, embarrassed, ashamed while having to pretend to be OK. I could also feel resentment at people who seemed happy together, while I felt so much loneliness and longing.

When in a relationship, the light-heartedness I would feel early on would rapidly disappear. I was busy in my own head and also trying to work out what was going on inside theirs. If I really liked them I may begin to feel insecure. As time went on my fear would be that a partner would discover how unlovable, damaged and unworthy I was. I felt I had to cover that up and try to be something different. I was managing myself, censoring myself in conversation, while attempting to appear laid-back but inside I was working very hard trying not to screw it up.

Those feelings of insecurity led to me going on numerous courses, retreats and even having years of therapy to work on myself. Maybe then I thought I would be good enough to fall in love with, maybe then I could have the kind of connection I yearned for?

My reasons for getting into a relationship were sometimes questionable. I was still looking for something outside of me to make me feel OK. At this point I still had no idea of what I would learn later, how life was an inside job. Sometimes I ended up in a relationship to avoid feeling the loneliness and to prove I was desired or desirable. Sometimes I was really keen on a partner but soon I would start fearing they were not that into me. I felt so damaged and critical of myself that it seemed impossible they could not be feeling critical of me with all my glaring faults. As the paranoia and insecurity would set in I would spend my days trying to work out what might be in their heads: did they like me, was something wrong, or what could it mean about our relationship if they said this or did that? Was it over, were they over me? Perhaps they felt me less present and wondered where the fun, light-hearted girl they first met had gone.

Another thing I would do once in a relationship would be to try to morph into what I thought they wanted me to be. It seemed preferable to showing the real me. As a result I would start to enjoy myself less and felt like I was losing myself; I wondered

'Why can't they just love me for who I am?' Do you know how hard it is to fake being OK - trying to come across as light, breezy, confident and worthy when underneath the surface you feel none of those things at all? I would not feel good and as a result would start to question the relationship. Could this person really be right for me if I felt this bad? I just wanted to feel relaxed and myself and for them to love me for who I was. The majority of my time was spent by me working out whether or not I wanted to be in the relationship instead of enjoying myself. Before long I had one foot in the relationship and one foot out.

The conversations in my head were very circular. I thought if I think about this hard enough I will get to the bottom of it, get to the correct answer to 'Is this the right person for me?' I would list all the pros and cons. Sometimes it felt clear it was a 'no' to the relationship. Then within minutes I would be imagining life alone forever, fearing I would never meet anyone ever again. I would start to doubt myself and I would override my wisdom (my quieter knowing) and my intellect would win. I would be back to square one again. My own personal logic at the time, without any evidence or proof of this helping, was to think my way out of problems. If I was not getting answers then I simply had to think about it harder.

In the area of relationship, I was scrambling around in the dark. I just kept hoping that one day this area would come good for me but feeling like I lacked the expertise to have a truly good relationship. I wanted it more than I wanted anything. The only thing I could think of was to work harder at it. I probably had more helpful ideas from my deeper knowing such as just be yourself or relax but in my usual way I would override those ideas.

In February 2015 I turned fifty! By then I had learnt something about how the mind works that had a massive impact on the way I saw life. As a result, my life started to feel simple and lighter having once felt serious and complicated. Surely there must be a clue there for my love life? So far it had not seemed to touch that area though. Or had it? One day I decided to do some internet dating. I scrolled through and was struck by the profile of one man. As I read his profile, about his philosophy on life, his favourite books, films, I found myself agreeing with every sentence. I wrote to tell him and then... nothing happened!

In June, four months after writing to him, I heard back! I was away on holiday when I received the message and we agreed to meet up for a drink when I got home. From the moment he wrote I had a different feeling about this. This time, thankfully it did not seem to make sense to me to overthink it. I just showed up to the date. We met in a pub and we had a great evening. It is the feeling of the date I can remember. No idea what we talked about but we sure did laugh. 'Do you want to do it again tomorrow?' he asked. 'Sure,' I said. We had a lovely time, why wouldn't I want to do that again? And so it began: the start of navigating a relationship differently. The start of listening to a deeper knowing. The start of something beautiful that six years on and now married, brings us both so much joy, happiness and gratitude every day, I still keep choosing it. I don't worry about the future or any of the things I used to spend my time contemplating. It is the NOW that I want to show up to because that is where the magic happens.

What used to feel like the very serious business of relationships doesn't anymore. It is playful and silly, fun and light. It has a completely different feel. How could it be that I stopped working so hard and it got easier, not harder? How could it be that when I ended up just being myself that I did not feel lost and misunderstood? In fact I felt like even I loved me! How could I love me when I had spent so much time trying to cover up the real me as I thought I was unlovable?

I felt so relieved and blessed that this time I sensed what to do and stopped trying to work it out in my head. I felt so grateful that it made sense to me to listen to the quiet voice within rather than using my intellect to navigate my relationship. I felt grateful that showing up as me without morphing into someone else gave me the opportunity to see I was loved and appreciated for who I was. I had always had issues with trust, fearing I had to be always on my guard in order to keep myself safe, and prevent someone from hurting me. Now I listen to my inner knowing, I trust myself to know what is or isn't OK for me. I feel strong and resilient. There are many other gifts when I show up to the relationship in the now rather than in my head. I am more light-hearted, funnier, I feel close, loving and connected. I fill up with feelings such as love, compassion and understanding.

My relationship journey has been a long and rocky road full of many serious and painful moments. Once I started to see my part in it – not in a blame-y kind of way but in a holy crap I did not see how I was getting in my own way kind of way – I took my own foot off the serious pedal, stopped squeezing the life out of relationships and it all started to flow. The joy and the pleasure squeezed out by my serious over-thinking flooded in and filled me up.

Wow! We Got Divorced

Janet Rhynie

I got married in what may be considered in some cultures as late in life. Up to thirty-seven, I'd studied, created a business, been appointed the first woman to sit on the board within a Pentecostal church, and led an interdenominational singles group. Life was good. Through it all, I had a constant companion who eventually became my husband. In 2007 we decided to get married. Why not? We had similar aspirational and inspirational views; we even became known as the 'Will and Jada Smith of the church'. I'd also spent a considerable amount of time and money on personal development. By then, I was a Master NLP (Neuro-Linguistic Programming) practitioner, had mastered the Emotional Freedom Technique, and utilised these and other techniques in my life and my work as a part-time probation officer and emotional wellbeing coach. Needless to say, I thought I was pretty switched on, self-aware and together.

I was happy to be married! Financially everything was split in two, we moved into our dream home, and I took the role of wife very seriously. My role model for this was my mother, so I went about doing what she had done, which was to put my father first.

This, however, began to take its toll on me. I felt I was withdrawing into myself to be 'the good wife'. I did not 'feel' as bright and shiny as I had before. Although I was laughing outside, I felt dull and grey inside, as if I was hiding my light. I remember noticing a year or so into my marriage that I was trying to be like her. But it felt so alien and unnatural to me. That was when I first noticed the expectations I had brought into the marriage of what I thought a husband and wife should be. I never even considered he would have his own expectations.

I recall us having an argument after we had attended a family event. It was a buffet-style meal, and so we had to get our food. When we got home, my husband was upset because I did not go to the table and get his food!! My response was, 'Why! Something wrong with your hands?' He was not amused.

Then, eighteen months into my marriage, something snapped. I was in the utility room, doing the laundry, screaming inside and thinking, 'Is this my life? Is this the way that marriage should be?' I was so unhappy, so miserable. Another thought then popped into my head, 'Well, he's a good guy, he's a good man, we get on. Well, let's just work at it. I would rather stay with him than be single.' This did not feel like the right course of action. However, I later came to understand that was the voice of my ego, doing its best to protect me.

2010 was the start of the parting of ways. I remember it clearly because that was when I decided to start learning about The Three Principles, and my husband started a course on strategic leadership. The goal was to combine what we learned in both courses to help us in our separate businesses. What seemed like a logical decision took me down a path I could never have foreseen. Was this wisdom? What I do know is I don't believe in coincidence and this was meant to happen. This arbitrary decision ended up taking us in very different directions.

The decision to learn about The Three Principles came about because I intended to teach it to others as a business programme and thought it would provide a more spiritual, holistic approach to both of our businesses. I had no idea of the impact The Three Principles would have upon me personally. The greater clarity I had about these spiritual principles, the more I started to rediscover myself. The insights felt like a weight lifted from my soul, and the light began shining brighter within. I began to see the person I'd been hiding to stay in the marriage. I began to understand that I was living in a thought-created reality. This led me to realise that my feelings of disillusionment, frustration and disappointment about my marriage had nothing to do with my husband. They came from expectations I placed upon myself and him about how I thought marriage should be. I saw all experience as creation.

The more I learned and understood, the further I drifted from my husband, both personally and professionally. He was focused on strategy, whilst I was focused more on the spiritual aspect of life. The Janet I had created over thirty-seven years and had taken so seriously was just an illusion – an ego I had created and then decided to live up to. The more I understood The Three Principles, the more this illusion of Janet faded, and the true spiritual essence, my true identity began to shine through.

I saw that I was no longer the Janet who had married in 2007. I couldn't tolerate pretending to be that person anymore as I felt like I was living a lie. My emerging spiritual core was taking the lead from the ego, and as such, the marriage started to break down.

After six years of marriage, I knew in my heart we were no longer compatible, but my ego decided I should work at the union. Upon reflection I could see this decision was taken from a place of fear. Fear of being judged by others. So I wanted to ensure I had tried everything to save it. In 2013 I decided the way to solve the issues we faced was to work at them. Hoping that The Three Principles would salvage our marriage, I chose to read *The Relationship Handbook: A Simple Guide to Satisfying Relationships* by Dr George Pransky (2014). This book reinforced that my feelings were coming from my thinking 100% of the time and that the feelings I had about my husband/my marriage were predominantly negative. Once again, ego took control, so I resorted to old techniques and tried to reframe my thoughts to see the relationship more positively. Phrases like 'It's just your thinking' and 'This will pass' became my mantras to deal with the negativity I was feeling.

Needless to say, this became tiring and almost a full-time job because I could see I was using The Three Principles as a technique to try to change my state of mind, and it didn't work.

In the space between frustrated thought and forced action, a different question arose. 'What would it be like if we were not together anymore?' The question was coming from a place of curiosity instead of needing to fix the marriage. There was a lightness about the question so that whatever the answer was, I knew I would be OK. It felt right.

I spoke to my husband about this. He knew something was not right with the marriage but did not know what to do. He agreed, and we decided on a trial separation. This coincided with him winning a contract that required him to live away from home. That was perfect, as it offered me the space to look at the marriage objectively. Constantly seeing my husband, I felt guilty, and the ego wanted to fix the situation. Without that constant thought, I was able to experience life guilt-free.

For the three months apart, I enjoyed the feeling of lightness, levity and clarity. This felt right! Once the contract was over, he returned home on a full-time basis. I knew life could not go back to the way it was, and I could not depend upon him getting contracts to live out our separate lives. At that moment, a new question arose, 'What if we got divorced?'

Again, as before, there was a lightness, levity and clarity in the question. This was my wisdom as I had not been trying to solve the problem of logically planning out the next steps. It felt right. In allowing wisdom to lead, I dared to have a conversation with my husband about divorce. There was no fear about having the conversation or what his response would be. Deep within me, this was the path to take.

And the rest, we shall say, is history. A great history. My ex-husband is now remarried, and I have met my soulmate!

'Forgiveness brings forth peace of mind. Without forgiveness, the road through life is paved with doubt and misery.' – Sydney Banks (1998)

People will say divorce is a stressful and challenging time in your life. In fact, research has shown divorce is in the top two of most stressful life events. It is topped only by the death of a loved one.

It was never my intention to divorce. I thought I would be married to one person forever, but slowly I lost myself in the marriage. I withdrew into myself, not knowing what the future held. It was as if I had wrapped myself in a cocoon. However, the ego was pushing to find a resolution, and that was when I felt stressed because I wanted to make things right.

Learning about The Three Principles was the catalyst to rediscover me. A metamorphosis was taking place inside, stripping away the old to reveal the new. This was when I heard the wisdom within the frustration, and I experienced calm and clarity. There was no doubt when I followed wisdom. As such, my experience of divorce was perfectly peaceful, following the path of wisdom.

To you reading this, if you find yourself in a marriage where you feel things are not working out, know your ego will try to take charge, trying to fix the situation. That is its job. You created it to be that way.

Forgive yourself because forgiveness brings clarity. You are doing the best you can with what you had at the time.

When the small quiet voice visits you amid your frustration and suggests something you had not logically thought of yourself – listen, for that is where peace lies.

Through this whole experience, you will emerge renewed, just like a butterfly emerging from its cocoon.

From Piss Artist to Abstract Artist...

Lucy Sheffield

I spent twenty-four years of my life hiding behind the drink. Not feeling good enough. Not feeling brave enough to show the real me. Not feeling like the real me could come out to play because no one understood me. I was a victim, but I didn't realise it. Hindsight is a wonderful thing. As I write this, I have been living a sober life for just over a year.

Do I have life all figured out now? Do I live in peace and harmony all of the time? Do I never have moments of craving that drink and wondering what life would be like if I just drank again sometimes?

Of course not – I am human. I have my wobbles, but they are a totally different experience than I have had before.

So, what changed for me?

For the last ten years I have been on a transformational journey of sorts, an internal journey if you will. I got to the age of thirty and I'd had enough of being the me I had created. I hated myself. I hated the person I had become, and I hated the way I showed up and treated others.

I wanted to change. I knew there was more to life. I knew I was ready to face things and explore and investigate. Delve deeper into me.

A lot of layers of the 'created' were shed, as I began to understand myself in a different way, at a deeper level than just this surface human who played at life. I began to realise I had a spiritual part to me as well, in fact I realised all of us do. That was a game changer for me. The missing piece of the puzzle.

So, over the years, I began to view life with a different set of lenses. I saw love and beauty in so many places that had seemed to be hidden from my view. I saw that we are all made up of love, and that we forget that a lot of the time and react from fear instead. When we don't know ourselves in this way we fear others too. When we fear others we act with defence. I had it set up that the world was against me, that it was out to get me. I thought life hated me and was never doing anything in my favour.

This fell away for me in so many areas in my life, and I began to grow and blossom as a much healthier, beautiful person who acted from love a lot more of the time.

But, and yes this is a big but! My drinking stayed. The one thing I wished I could see differently. The one thing I wished that wouldn't have such a tight grip on me. The one big thing I had wanted to change about me in the first place stayed still, stubborn and standing its ground. It wouldn't leave me. Or perhaps I wouldn't leave it.

An unhealthy relationship between me and those deep red bottles of poison remained. I could justify my actions until the cows came home. After all, I didn't hurt anyone. Yes I admit in the past I had been verbally horrid with my ex. But I had seen something in life that now meant I didn't feel so angry or defensive. Surely that meant I could drink. I was only harming myself, and of course that didn't really count or matter. I was fine.

It wasn't until I began dating another woman and we had been together five months that I started to get suspicious. It was a hard pill to swallow, but I had to face the reality – which was I couldn't bring myself to have sober sex. Anytime that seemed to be on the cards I would make an excuse about being tired or needing a shower or anything to get out of it. I would even make myself drink on nights when I'd had such a bad hangover the last thing I wanted to do was get drunk again. But it was the better option than facing sober sex. I was too scared. Too scared that I wasn't confident in the bedroom, too scared I wasn't good enough for her. Too scared of all the things I thought I was expected to do to hold up this image of what being a lesbian was.

And of course I knew this was all about me. It had nothing to do with her. But was I brave enough to face this? I didn't think so. It was hard enough just letting my own mind go there. I could never say it out loud to another human, let alone the woman I was in the relationship with.

So I just let it carry on for a bit, hiding behind the drink, pretending it was all OK. Until one day she called me to say she had cheated on me. And boy did that rock my world. I had no clue it was coming. I felt stupid, used, upset, angry, hurt. All of those things you would expect to feel.

However, I had lots of support around me and somehow found myself stumbling through those next few days/weeks. I ended things with her and very quickly realised here was my chance to do this drink thing. I had asked the universe only a few weeks previously to show me a way around all of this drink stuff. I knew I was ready. I knew it was time.

I mean, if it was down to me, I do have to say I wish the universe had perhaps been a little gentler on me. It's hard dealing with someone cheating. But it made me take the bull by the horns, slip into my big girl pants and decide it was my time to be a single, sober Lu. Here was my chance to step into that final straw of learning something about me.

And here we are thirteen months on. What I would like to share with you next is how much I have transformed beyond belief or words in those thirteen months. To try to portray to you what it is I've seen and continue to see is a challenge when I only have words... but here goes.

I have seen that I can trust life. Even when things come up that seem to be unfair, hard for us to take on and a massive struggle to get through. I can still trust life.

I have seen that confidence is a state of mind. I have seen that I can trust myself, and that every single one of us has that same wisdom that we can rely on. As humans we so often ask for opinions from others, we want to rely on things outside of us all of the time. We forget that we can rely on ourselves. That we have gut feelings and heart-led choices come up for us. We wobble and think, 'yeah, but not here'.

I have seen that I am good enough. That I am enough. That every single one of us is enough. We are built to thrive in this playground of life, but we forget that.

I have seen that certainty (without the huge splash of arrogance) in our own selves impacts others. When we have clarity and confidence, we attract others. They gravitate towards us, because we are shining our truth light so bright.

All we want in life is to feel a version of peace, happiness, joy, freedom, or whatever word makes sense to us. We go round and round in circles trying to find it, missing the simple fact that it resides inside of us, and always has done.

I love spending my days writing, painting or helping others achieve their dreams with creativity. We all have creative flow running through us, and for years I blocked myself from being able to express or articulate this. Since quitting the drink I now have nothing in my way, nothing to hold my hand. So I had to learn to trust in myself, to believe in me.

I now spend my days helping other women to see this in themselves too. Following our heart desires brings nothing but a deep sense of peace, joy and all the love and happiness in the world. Why would we fill our days doing anything but that which makes our heart sing?

We all have a creative purpose. We are all meant to live a life we love. We are all here to help and impact others by allowing those creative talents to shine from our very core.

We can trust in life. We can trust in ourselves. We can achieve anything!

The Story of Me

Christine Friend

My first memories of me, of how people perceived me, and by extension what I knew of myself, were that I was clever but I was a procrastinator. In fact, 'procrastination' was the first big word I ever learnt.

I am sure that 'you're so clever' was said in the absolute belief that the words were encouraging and confidence boosting, and for a while they were. It is so natural as a parent to encourage little children, to hang on to every word, praise every new skill, be amazed at every scribble. Any parent will know, without even thinking, the words we use to encourage: 'that's so clever', 'clever girl', 'amazing', 'you are brilliant'.

Somehow over time this innocent label I'd been given became part of my identity. I wasn't just a child who sometimes did above-average things; no, I was a clever person. This small, some might say semantic, difference was seismic to me. It was something I took very seriously. I had confused a description of the way I behaved with who I was. I now had a persona that I felt I had to secure, protect and maintain. What started out as a winning formula, one that was helpful and supportive, became a noose around my neck.

During my primary school years, I had evidence to support my persona. I got sent to the year above to choose my reading books. I often finished work quickly and ended up helping others that hadn't got it yet. I was sent to stretch classes with the headmaster. It all confirmed to me what I already knew. However, in my confidence there was no room for doubt or vulnerability. When I found something more difficult, it was hard to ask for help – I was the helper after all. When I couldn't immediately get something right, I would pretend I had lost homework or not finished. If it wasn't done, it couldn't be marked as wrong and I would not have to face denting my persona. When I was bored or struggling, I would begin to cast about for someone to blame for my feelings and more often than not the targets were the teachers. I would use my intellect to try to outsmart them, make them look silly by getting a laugh out of the class, lead them into interminable circular conversations that wasted more time and generally adopted a 'too cool for school' attitude. Contentment was being right but happiness was proving someone else wrong.

Moving to secondary school, things escalated even further. In the first new humanities lesson I found that I had already done the whole topic in my previous school. I waited until class had finished and told the teacher. I still remember clearly what she said – 'Well, you will just have to wait a couple of terms until everyone else has caught up.' I could feel the injustice of having to do nothing, of having to wait again when I had been promised that secondary school would be challenging and I could feel my imagined persona jumping to my rescue and trying to defend my right to have my cleverness noticed. In that confused way we fall into so often when our ego gets defensive, no reasonable, clear-thinking solution came to me, instead it looked like a solid idea to just try to disrupt every class. If they couldn't teach me then I would refuse to learn... and so it began.

Within a couple of weeks, I was on report and stayed there for almost the next six years. I must have held the record for the number of times my parents were called in. Each meeting or school report ended with the same words: 'You are not fulfilling your potential.' In my defence it looked logical to fight those who seemed to be the source of my unhappiness. What I didn't see then was that all the time and energy spent attacking them was slowly but surely attacking me. Each teacher just wrote me off and went onto a new class, but I had to live with the consequences of not working and learning forever.

I had a bit of insight around the start of my GCSE years; I realised that I was only hurting myself and I could go back to school in the new year with a fresh start and work hard and ace my exams. Unfortunately, my identity was still aligned with protecting the old idea of me and so I remained on alert for any slight or danger that might open me up to being caught out as less than clever. So, when the teachers began to notice my exemplary behaviour, they all began to comment: 'Where is the old girl that we know so well?', 'This is unusual, I wonder if you can keep it up?', etc. I heard this not as encouragement but as a sign that they did not want me to change so within weeks I had crept back behind my armour plating and I didn't do any more work for the next two years.

So, the identity of me seemed set, and the school couldn't wait to be shot of me so wouldn't let me stay on. I went to college aimlessly but did nothing as it was all too easy. I went to work aimlessly, and drifted into accountancy, then teaching adults, then coaching. Always in the background of doing very well in work I suffered from a nagging self-doubt. Who would I, could I have been if I had fulfilled my potential and studied and done a degree? This led to a version of impostor syndrome known to many. I stayed alert in conversations to see if I could add something intelligent or prove that I knew the answer. I remained hard to teach as I always needed to be right, to be one step ahead of the class. I spent lots of brain bandwidth on worrying about what people thought of me. It was always easier to do nothing rather than something that might be judged as less than, so that judgement would not shatter the illusion I gripped so tightly.

Through years of personal growth work for my coaching practice, a major insight became clear: I had wasted forty years having me on my mind. I saw that I had spent many years thinking I was in a different boat to other people. I held on to my story of school woes and it made it impossible for me to ever get over my hang-ups. What I had missed was that, as a human being with the same magnificent psychological system as everyone else, we were all in the same boat. All struggling with the same illusions and misunderstandings about where our true self lies.

Breaking the domino effect of all this misunderstanding has given me true freedom. I am unique and... an utterly ordinary human being at the same time. I started life with a diamond of pure potential. I took innocent labels and plastered them over my diamond. I then made many meanings, and stories that I dropped on top like a huge turd. I wasted forty years polishing that turd. Sprinkling glitter on it to hide it from others and keeping me on my mind to stay alert in case anyone came close to uncovering that turd.

I remember in one training becoming really upset as I got closer to feeling the depth of my true self and I said, 'What if I find who I really am, and I don't like that person?' I had accepted an identity given to me by other people and held on to that as 'me' without stopping to question or update software that had been installed in childhood. It was a relief to no longer have to waste time on taking myself so seriously, because I had made it all up in the first place!

I now have the freedom to know that who I really am is pure, endless potential, joy and love. Seeing through all of this has taken so much thinking off my mind. Now I don't have to protect the idea of me, I don't need to stay on alert for slights to my ego and I don't have to prove myself all the time. The key change is that I have gone from needing to be right about everything (just ask my family), to relishing not knowing.

When I don't know: I listen better. When I don't know: I am more curious to understand. When I don't know: I am able to experiment, fail and really learn. Not knowing is where openness, curiosity and growth start.

I still have moments, blind spots, where I don't see that truth. I feel insecure about people judging my work; I make assumptions about what is possible for me or others. But I have also got better at spotting the signposts that I am off track and my illusory ego is fighting back. I know, beyond all else, that I am OK and that approval, appreciation and being liked are just lovely side effects of living a life secure in my wellbeing that shines through for others to see.

Guided

Tania Elfersy

'When you return from your maternity leave, we'll want you to visit our customers in California and Taiwan more often.'

I nodded dutifully and stared at the two men leading my annual work review, both of them fathers. I was eight months' pregnant with my first child, and was feeling a little uncomfortable with my belly squashed against the meeting room table, when a wave of calm spread over me.

Leaving the corporate world would be easy after all.

'Do you see this?' I asked my boss a few weeks later, pointing to my belly. 'This means I'm going to have a baby soon and you're going to have to stop throwing so much work at me! We've already found my maternity-leave replacement and it's going to be fine when she takes over!'

My body told me to say that.

It had been sending me signs (symptoms) for months that my workload was incompatible with the very ancient task at hand – bringing a baby into this world.

Building my career in the dot.com boom had served me well, but I was ready to stand down as the breadwinner and turn my attention to motherhood.

Just in time, my husband's business took off and started flourishing. As a new family, we were blessed and provided for.

Six years and three children later, I sought a gentle re-entry into the (paid) workforce, and I had an idea to create a gift book for new mums to support them as they journeyed through motherhood. I co-authored the book with a dear friend and then set off alone on a self-publishing adventure.

The creation of the book evolved with ease – inspiration appeared at every step. Once out in the world, the book picked up four international book awards, and received loving reviews from mums and the media. In terms of sales, I picked an ambitious number out of the air and got to work to meet my target.

I took a business course to learn more about online sales and marketing and one of the exercises we were asked to do involved sending out a questionnaire to our friends to discover what they thought our strengths were.

'You're passionate!'

'Determined!'

'You set goals and achieve them!' shared my friends.

That sounded right at the time. It certainly matched a story I could patch together about myself, and here I was, publishing my first book, picking up accolades – surely, I was on a roll?

But I wasn't. Nothing about selling my books felt in flow – I was always seeking another expert to tell me what step-plan to implement.

I was putting in a lot of effort and seeing very few results. The unsold boxes of books stacked wherever they could be hidden, weighed heavily on my heart.

Once, I had known my value in the workplace and had watched my salary grow. Now I was juggling motherhood and my own business, and I felt that I was floundering in both.

'I'm a failure. I'm not enough,' said the voice in my head (but no one else). That voice would make me cry.

I thought I should work even harder, put in more late hours. But that didn't help sell my books, and my health began to suffer.

I started getting sick often, which was unusual for me. Then I started getting migraines, skin problems, night sweats and terrible mood swings. I didn't understand what was going on, but I felt that I was falling apart.

If only I could implement some of those online marketing plans like I was supposed to, then my business would take off.

If only I would write more often in my gratitude journal and repeat my mantras, then I would manifest my desires.

If only I could meditate, my days would be calmer.

If only the acupuncturist, or those supplements, or those potions could cure me, then I'd be happy!

I kept searching outside of me for THE THING that would make me feel like myself again.

I'd been suffering with my symptoms for a few years when I tuned into a webinar and heard that many women in their forties experienced what could be described as *PMS on steroids*. My ears pricked up! I was forty-five and that was exactly how I felt! It was as if every month I experienced two weeks of PMS – from ovulation to menstruation. That was the first time I'd heard about perimenopause, the period of change (which can last up to ten years) that occurs before the onset of menopause.

Like many women, I'd entered my forties not thinking about THE CHANGE! I'd thought that menopause took place on average at fifty-one (it does) and that, somehow, I would have nothing to do with it before then. Yet, just as in our teenage years we don't develop our adult breasts and a regular period overnight, so it is at midlife: change takes time.

Learning about perimenopause made me feel a little less crazy, because it offered a framework for my symptoms. It also offered hope that there was ONE THING that could cure them all – if I just balanced my hormones! However, as I read more about conventional and alternative hormonal treatments, nothing made sense.

If my body had known what to do to develop from a baby, to a girl, to a teenager, to a woman and then (in my case) also to a mother, why would it not know how to progress through menopause? Did the intelligence of my body stop come midlife? Did my hormones start getting it wrong? Was the depletion of oestrogen that all women experience as they approach menopause a divine mistake?

In the Bible, we learn that Sarah, a Jewish matriarch, laughed when she was told she would give birth. She was postmenopausal and knew what that meant! As did those who wrote her story, and as it was assumed the readers would, too. This is not the only evidence around to convince us that postmenopausal women have roamed the earth for at least thousands of years. The idea that women suffer come midlife because they never used to live beyond forty is a myth! Over the ages, child mortality rates were high and this contributed to low AVERAGE life expectancy.

So, what goes on during perimenopause and menopause that makes so many women experience such a wide variety of symptoms? What was creating my symptoms?

From my ongoing research into perimenopause and menopause, and from talking to women around me, I got the sense that something inside me could lead to the cure.

Then one day, I had an insight:

If I didn't have unresolved issues, I wouldn't have PMS. And since I was creating my unresolved issues through taking my thinking about certain things in my life seriously, I could also not take that thinking seriously. In fact, that would be easier. Then I wouldn't have issues and I wouldn't have PMS.

In that moment, I understood that no matter what thought came to mind, whether it was 'I've always met my goals' or 'I'm a failure', I didn't have to take any of them seriously. All thoughts were temporary blips of energy that could only make me feel a certain way if I believed they revealed truth, rather than an illusion of it.

To my surprise, following that insight, not only did my PMS disappear, all my other physical symptoms vanished too, within days.

Perimenopause/menopause is a sensitive time, just like our teenage years, pregnancy and postpartum. When our bodies are busy with change, they have much less tolerance for a life out of balance. I'd thought that my symptoms were a sign of malfunction. But in fact, they were an expression of my body's brilliance – the same brilliance that had guided me during my first pregnancy, years before.

My body had wanted me to take life less seriously! It didn't matter that I didn't reach a sales target, that my career once looked different, that many people, including me, used to hold on to a story of who I was and how life should turn out. None of that was important. Because no matter what is going on, joy and lightness are always my default (as they are yours). That is what my body wanted me to learn at midlife, because it is this under-standing that will protect us as we age.

The Light Side of Cancer

Elaine Hilides

When I was diagnosed with breast cancer in 2008, I almost expected it. I was diagnosed with the same cancer as my mother, at the same age she had been. Was there something in my unconscious expectation? Who knows?

But I knew that I wasn't my mother and my journey would be different. Back in 2008, I was a Neuro-Linguistic Programming (NLP) Master Practitioner, a Thought Field Therapy (TFT) Practitioner and Hypnotherapist, and I pulled all these skills together to deal with the diagnosis and the treatment. My mother's cancer had spread to her spine and she died six years after her initial diagnosis. If any intrusive thoughts popped up about this happening to me, I techniqued them into infinity and beyond. I used to visualise a team of men travelling through my body with brooms and brushes, sweeping and cleaning my body on the inside. Although why an imaginary team of men seemed less weird than visualising my cells doing what they are designed to do, I have no idea.

I felt that it was time to walk my talk and I did. I got through the operations mentally, if not physically, unscathed and I didn't dwell on any fears of what might happen next.

And then, in 2009, I was introduced to a new understanding of the mind, of life, and I realised how tightly I'd been holding on to being well. I could see how I'd been playing the part of someone who could control emotion and thought, imagining that I could keep fear at bay through the force of my will.

And now I could let go.

What a relief. I didn't need to control my thoughts and, as it was futile to try, I could just let thought flow through me.

And, so, when I was diagnosed with breast cancer again in 2020, it wasn't scary. It just was. When I was called in to get the results, it wasn't a surprise. In fact, I was so sure that I had cancer again, when my partner and I entered the room and I saw two other people in the room with the consultant, I laughed. 'Ah,' I said, 'this isn't going to be news I want to hear, is it?' 'No,' my consultant said gravely as she broke the news that I had cancer and clearly wondered what other issues I must have as I wasn't upset or shocked.

In the years since the first diagnosis, I hadn't worried that cancer might come back and, now that it had, I celebrated that it had taken thirteen years to resurface and that it was a small tumour. I didn't have any thoughts about 'fighting' cancer, 'winning a battle' or any of the other phrases that people use. Cancer hadn't happened 'to' me, it was part of me. These were my cells that had gone rogue, after all.

Seeing this led to two big insights. The first was that I could still love my body despite what was happening to it and the second was that whatever was happening was only happening to my body. It wasn't happening to me. My essence, my soul, my spirit, or whatever you might call your source, couldn't be touched and this led to a feeling of peace.

Yes, I don't really want any more bits and pieces cut off but I don't need to worry about whether that might happen. Inside I'm still the same as I was pre-cancer, the same as I was pre-school in fact. I guess this is why if you ask a seventy-year-old how they feel, they often answer, 'the same as I did when I was twenty-one'.

And this time around there was no reframing the situation or sending any unwanted thoughts out into space or employing an army of virtual male cleaners. I was able to be as peaceful, or as manic, as I am every other day. Nothing about the situation frightened me and, hand on heart, I really didn't have a moment's fear about the diagnosis or any potential prognosis. Suffering really is optional.

I was so unaffected by the whole process that I was told by two different sonographers, in two different hospitals, that I was just too calm. What were they going to do to me, I asked? As far as I knew, ultrasounds were painless. But hospital staff are so used to people feeling fear that I was an anomaly. But what are people fearing in that moment? Unless they're pathologically frightened of machines, it's a quick and painless procedure. What they're frightened of is what they think the process represents, a fear of the disease rather than the ultrasound, a fear of what might happen in the future and isn't it wonderful that we have no idea what will happen in the future.

It's a strange thing when you have a diagnosis. Some people get very serious and are confused that you aren't wailing and tearing your hair out. Well, it's hardly worth doing that; you could opt for chemotherapy and get the job done. Other people talk about how brave you are when you aren't crying into your coffee. Brave? I'm not tackling a gunman, I'm just going for a long sleep while lots of skilled people cut out the tumour and rearrange my body. Some people even get a little upset that you're not upset – after all, they say, you do have 'cancer', in their most serious voice.

Cancer is one of those loaded words, isn't it? If you rearranged the letters and said that you had crane no one would bat an eyelid. This demonstrates that the feeling doesn't come from the word but what the word represents to an individual. To someone who hasn't been personally touched by cancer, the word may not be as alarming as it would be to someone who has had the disease or lost someone close to them from the disease.

For many people cancer represents the dark side of life and they're confused when I talk about being happy with cancer. Now, I wasn't dancing in puddles that I *had* cancer but I was very happy *despite* having cancer.

And, unlike feeling fear, which normally has a reason, imagining a thing that you think might happen, I can be happy for no reason at all. Happiness is built in. Experts tell us that we are born with two innate fears, the fear of falling and the fear of loud noises, and every other fear is constructed whereas happiness is innate. Happiness comes with the package and the only reason that we don't feel happy is when we get lost in thought.

And the strange thing is that I had such little thought about having cancer that when people asked how my recovery was going, I had to pause for a minute to consider what they were saying. What recovery? From what? It really does slip my mind that I'd had cancer at all, let alone twice.

My cancer journey is both over and ongoing. There are scans and appointments in the future and, whilst this chapter is closed, I'm not sure what the rest of the book contains.

And so what? I don't have to think about what might happen in the future. I don't have to conjure up scary scenarios that aren't happening here in this moment and then experience the emotion that these thoughts have created.

I just have to take this journey, like every journey, step by step, just focusing on where my feet land in this moment.

And I'm free to do a happy little dance wherever my feet land.

A Message of Hope

Carol Boroughs

'"Hope" is the thing with feathers
That perches in the soul...' – Emily Dickinson (1891)

The headache was there when I woke up.

'It will be OK,' I told myself, 'Only a few more hours until the final exam.'

My body was tense; not even the hot shower helped. I could feel the muscles in my skull getting tighter as though I were physically trying to squish my brain to shut up my mind. Somehow it seemed to work for a while. Perhaps the pain of the headache caused by the tension was enough distraction. As a younger woman I might have pulled a corner of a damaged fingernail out of the nail bed. That certainly hurt enough to distract. But not that day: I had to get through the final exam of my degree. Undertaking a part-time degree in my forties with two young children was no small undertaking and I was not about to give up now.

It passed in a blur. It was done. By the time I got home my whole body ached. My nervous system was on high alert. The light hurt my eyes and each sound reverberated through every nerve ending. My head still pounded and my heart hammered inside my chest. This was not anticipatory anxiety for the exam but terror of the resurfacing memories that I was attempting to suppress. I got myself inside. I sensed this episode was going to be a bad one. It had been triggered a few days before by something I had seen on television. My go-to techniques which were usually so helpful hadn't really worked. If I had allowed the memory to come unchecked, I feared the unfolding might have been overwhelming and unpredictable, preventing me from doing the exam. So, I just held on as best I could. Somehow on this occasion I had delayed the inevitable tsunami of post-traumatic memories that flooded me the moment I turned the lock on the bathroom door and sank to my knees on the tiled floor. I was instantly transported back in time, reliving a violent event from the past.

Sometimes the flashbacks were relatively short-lived. I could go long intervals without being triggered but at times they provoked a reactionary period of depression or drove me to seek despairingly for more techniques or more healing. Disturbed sleep and nightmares had also been part of the picture for so long they had become normalised for me. I always considered myself fortunate that I didn't suffer as badly as others and that my healing journey had led me to some amazing healers and therapies that helped me function well in the world. So much so that I studied and qualified in a number of different therapeutic disciplines and specialised in helping men and women living with trauma. Survivors of childhood abuse, domestic violence, war, multiple bereavements and rape. Each life story unique, each soul seeking to understand and heal.

Yet there remained a deeply held belief that I was essentially wounded, that I was broken beyond repair because I could not go back in time and change the past. The perceived wisdom in the therapeutic field was that the next best option was to heal over the wound and learn to live with the scars. My own experience, and that of many of my clients, reinforced that belief over and over again. Trauma seemed to be stored in the body and the mind, perhaps even in the soul. It would surface piece by piece and from time to time, giving the wounded an opportunity to feel, touch, explore, understand and heal it. But the relief was temporary. It would resurface in a different shape and form, reconfigured with new scar tissue. I have met many people who have completely given up on healing their trauma because the pain of the therapeutic intervention is too much. Talking therapies that examined the past could inadvertently re-traumatise. Even the gentlest and most skillful of body work has the potential to trigger emotional pain.

Then I stumbled across the understanding at the heart of all the stories in this book, The Three Principles. In quick succession I had a series of profound realisations.

I had heard similar words many times before. People would say, the past does not exist, live in the Now. I would listen and quietly, sometimes angrily, think – yeah, easy for you to say; you haven't been through what I've been through and your mind doesn't terrorise you with memories hijacked by a transient sound or fragrance when you least expect it.

However, as Sydney Banks says, the understanding is not in the words but beyond them. The realisation of truth occurs from within through insight and a shift in understanding.

As the insight was realised – *the past does not exist except in my own thoughts* – there was a natural reflex action away from thoughts about the past. It wasn't something I did or had to learn. Just like we don't have to learn a technique for pulling our hand away from a hot stove. A natural falling away of thoughts about the past happened. I had no flashbacks for about three years. I felt incredibly light, free.

I saw how I had innocently been re-traumatising myself via old thought, contaminating my experience of this moment, of reality. In addition, I had been responding to those thoughts as though they were telling me something real and true about myself. Suddenly, the events of the past were seen as not existing anymore, unable to hold any emotional charge. When those old memories arise now, as they do only from time to time, my relationship to them is so radically changed that they no longer scare me. It is just like knowing that the movie is not real, just images on a screen.

Sydney Banks (1998) says:

'The intensity and importance of such events dissipates as we see that the past is no longer a reality, but a memory carried through time via our thoughts'

As layers of thought and belief about myself dropped away, a second insight was revealed.

A deep sense of knowing arose that I was unbroken, never wounded at all. My true nature was uncovered as the thought fell away and my spiritual essence was revealed – completely whole, unbroken.

Effortlessly my life became lighter and less serious.

There was a period of integration and recalibration. So much energy was freed up because I was no longer having to carry the emotional baggage of the past that I went through a period of not being able to sleep more than three or four hours a night but also not needing to! The serious business of fixing myself was over when I saw that old thinking for what it was.

Another radical change was my work. I could see how going back into the past to fix something was unnecessary at best and painful at worst. I began sharing The Three Principles with people, pointing them towards their wholeness. While I cannot give a person insight, this gentle conversation helps people look in a different direction and uncover something fundamentally true about the human experience. It feels very different to sit with someone who is exploring your brokenness and trying to fix it, than it does to be with someone who really sees your wholeness and helps you uncover it for yourself. Being present with someone who knows that you do not need to be fixed can act like one tuning fork causing another to vibrate at the same frequency.

Even long-standing problems that have existed for years can shift with one change in thought because the problems were created through thought in the first place. For other people, change is slower and more incremental, but the potential exists for everyone because the truth of our essential nature applies equally to all.

If you are currently weighed down by past trauma or are struggling with some other serious challenge, I would love for you to feel the hope for transformation in my story.

On that night in the bathroom, all I could hope for was a miracle.

In the words of Sydney Banks (1998):

'There are those in this world who believe miracles do not exist. I can assure such sceptics that they do. With hope and faith as beacons, anything can happen.'

Taking the Self-help Universe Seriously

Ivalo A. Arnfjord

I was born and raised in South Greenland, in a small city called Qaqortoq. I grew up as the oldest of four siblings. The reason I felt I needed to get into the self-help universe was that I had a couple of traumas in my childhood and adolescence.

One of the first terrifying experiences I remember was being sexually assaulted when I was nine years old. Unfortunately, I was also raped when I was nineteen. I was lost, depressed, lonely, blamed myself, felt shame and locked myself away from the rest of the world. I escaped from my dark feelings and drank a lot with my friends. I couldn't have the healthy relationship with men I longed for. Back then, there was not much help available in my hometown. There were no psychologists and the social workers were not helpful. When I finally opened up about my traumas to a woman I knew, she said to me that it was partially my fault I was raped, because I opened the door to that man. I believed what she said, and later she introduced me to Al-Anon* groups and a book, *You Can Heal Your Life* by Louise Hay (1984).

---

*Al-Anon are support groups for friends and families of alcoholics.

That was the beginning of my journey to find myself and seek the meaning of life. I loved everything from the self-help/new age/spirituality sections in bookstores. To me the new world was an inspiring and never-ending exploration. For the next twenty years or so I followed and admired many spiritual and self-help teachers such as Louise Hay (positive affirmations), Doreen Virtue (angel oracle cards), Debbie Ford (shadow work), Dr Madan Kataria (laughter yoga), Dr Mikao Usui (reiki healing), Neale Donald Walsch, Rhonda Byrne (author of *The Secret*) and many more. I practised the soul voice method, when I was alone in the mountains or near the ocean. I spent many hours doing different kinds of meditation, both guided and silent. I did emotional freedom technique (tapping) when I needed to get away from my dark feelings or if I was physically ill.

While my adventure into the self-help universe was wonderful, I still didn't really feel healed. I felt that I was broken inside, and that I was not whole. If there had been a self-help university, I would have been one of the top students. One of my biggest dreams was to open a self-help/spirituality bookshop where I could sell different kinds of books, for example with themes like spirituality, healing, religion, meditation, angel cards, crystals and so on.

When I was twenty-nine years old, I finally had the opportunity to see a psychologist, who helped me for about five years. During this time, I kept working on myself, by doing emotional cleansing, which involved talking about my feelings. I tried hard to forgive the people who had hurt me in the past. I tried to help myself, but felt I needed an outside resource to help me have a good life. I wanted to improve myself all the time, because I unconsciously believed that my soul was damaged and needed help to recover from my past traumas.

The different tools, techniques and methods greatly helped me put my life into perspective in a more positive way. I enjoyed them and experienced many beautiful things. All these different experiences with my attempt to help myself, lasted only temporarily.

Sight from within

One day at the beginning of 2018 I talked to my sister about how I wanted to write a book with my friend Tina, about the importance of improving self-love and working with one's inner child. Her response was not what I expected, she wasn't as thrilled as I thought she would have been and said something like: 'I don't control things like that anymore.' That sentence sparked something in me. I thought, 'Wow, what was that?' Then it made me curious – because she used to be on the same wavelength as me when it came to the self-help universe.

During a flight from Denmark to Greenland, I wanted to relax and listen to the audio book *Dit selvhelbredende sind* (*Your Self-Healing Mind*) by Mette Louise Holland (2017), which my sister Louise and my friend Arnajaraq had recommended. I put on my noise-cancelling headphones and turned it on, relaxed and just listened to it. I think I was in a kind of sleeping state while I was listening, then I had my first INSIGHT!! I saw myself from above, I was observing the landscape and a valley nearby. I saw my life metaphorically; in the landscape I saw a 'tube' which I had created during my whole life and that tube symbolised how I had controlled my thoughts, for example, by thinking positive thoughts, visualising and attracting what I desired in my life. I realised that the tube had not helped me, but instead had restrained me! Then I came out of it, and I descended into a valley, in between mountain cliffs, but instead of falling and hitting the ground I floated on air. I was drifting in the air when I experienced a revelation and finally understood something deep!

I realised that everything is energy. I had trapped myself unconsciously and innocently in my own personal mind and had not known that I had always been connected to the universal mind. I had learnt that I had to develop myself and work hard to create a life that I wanted. I didn't know how I was part of the universal mind. I had understood spirituality intellectually. When I fell and was out of this self-created tube, I realised that I was FREE, I was out of my own control, out of my personal mind. I didn't even have to feel trust. I didn't have to work hard to feel peace and happiness. I was just there, in the air. Just being. What a natural feeling. I knew that it was enough to just be. I didn't need to have control over my life anymore, because life has my back. Life is part of me. I am part of life. I knew that this invisible power, invisible force or universal mind took care of me. What a relief, I thought: I will never be the same again! It gave me such a feeling of peace. I didn't even have to move. Everything just stopped. I WOKE up to life. I realised that I have always been and always will be whole. I took my headphones off and said to my former colleague who sat beside me: 'I have misunderstood everything! I finally got it! Now I know!' I knew she didn't understand it. But I had changed.

Innate Health

I had many insights after that; it was truly healing from within; it was amazing. Even though I had dreamed of creating a self-help/spirituality bookshop, I couldn't be serious about that dream anymore after my insights. It is a big thing to give up a dream like that, because the most important thing I saw was that I would rather have other people get an opportunity to understand their own inner wisdom/inner health/inner source.

God knows how many self-help books I have read, many of which helped me, but it was always temporary. I had understood intellectually what the different writers were writing about, but after my first insights, I understood them in my heart. I couldn't keep all the books I had collected through the years, so I got rid of them, because I didn't need to read other people's insights and get my answers there. I stopped going to my psychologist because I knew I was healed from within. I couldn't be a follower anymore. I realised that I can only find answers that are designed for me through my own insights, within me. It is like the last piece in a giant puzzle finally found its place. I couldn't be serious anymore about fixing myself. I felt an enormous difference between an ego searching the self-help world and a world open to universal wisdom!

From Fear to Lightness

Lara Fares

'Life is like any other contact sport. You may encounter hardships of one sort or another. Wise people find happiness not in the absence of such hardships, but in their ability to understand them when they occur.'
– Sydney Banks (1998)

One of life's great mysteries is why some people have an insight during their lifetime and others don't. Why do some words resonate with some people, giving them an 'a-ha' moment, yet aren't even noticed by others? Why do some people hear things in a certain way while others interpret them differently? Perhaps by sharing my story you will hear something new.

One thing I'm sure of is that an insightful experience changes the way one responds to life's daily occurrences. I myself had one such experience on a very lonely evening in my hotel room whilst visiting Philadelphia, USA in 2017.

I was dropping my daughter off at university for the first time. She had never left home before for more than two weeks. In a few days I was due to return home to London and leave her in this foreign city within a huge country where she would be spending the next four years away from me. I found myself feeling very low. I was engrossed in imagining the near future – arriving home without either of my daughters (twins who were both beginning their studies in the USA). For the first time since they were born,

I would not be seeing them every day, I would not be by their side and they would have to manage their own lives.

Moreover, my sister had just been diagnosed with pancreatic cancer and had been told she didn't have long to live. I was left feeling scared and anxious.

The world suddenly looked very dark. I struggled to find any silver linings. My fear, anxiety and loneliness surrounded me, consuming all my thoughts.

That evening, while browsing YouTube to find some nurturing video clips which would calm my nerves, I came across Sydney Banks and The Three Principles. While watching I noticed a growing curiosity of what these Principles could be and how they might add to my life. I didn't know it at the time, but clicking on this video was about to change my life forever.

It was my moment to have an insight!

Listening to Sydney Banks talk resonated with my soul. It felt as though he was awakening something within me, as if I had once heard his words before but they had been buried away for years. I felt peace take over my body and mind – a huge sense of relief. It was a sensation I had never felt before.

I felt a profound sense of safety, realising that nothing and no one could ever really hurt me. When one feels so grounded, everything else suddenly seems very light, with even the ugliest of what life has to offer no longer seeming ugly, but simply different to what you call beautiful.

If only I could bottle this lightness, this feeling!

I felt euphoric. I wanted to call everyone I knew and ask them if they had heard of a man called Sydney Banks and his Three

Principles. In fact, I have been doing just that since that night. I couldn't bear to think that there were people I know and love who hadn't heard of Banks and his work

However, as I mentioned before, words don't touch every person identically. The Three Principles resonate with every individual differently. Is there a reason some people have their insightful experience or 'a-ha' moment when exposed to certain stimuli, and others don't? I felt reassured by the fact that having this insightful moment and not ever having experienced it are seconds apart. This highlighted that my feelings of loneliness and darkness were triggered by what my mind was focusing on – my daughters moving away from home and losing my sister to cancer. The situations themselves didn't cause my state, it was my thoughts which did.

My sister was still alive, she was still here. My thoughts were transporting me into a future hypothetical state that, at the time, was non-existent.

Becoming aware that every single one of us has a divine part to us, which is unshakeable, has helped me shift to a much higher vibration and feel much healthier emotions. It reassured me to focus on this divine part within my sister, regardless of whether she was aware of it or not. I knew that it was indestructible, even to cancer.

When we look at life through these lenses, things become easier to handle. Of course, life still throws us challenges, but they just become easier to overcome.

Back in my Philadelphia hotel room, I slept so well that night and found myself noticing that everything felt lighter the next morning when I visited my daughter on campus. I was spontaneously smiling more, and not carrying my heavy irrational thoughts with me. Noticing the pleasures of simply living in the present moment with my lovely daughter and focusing on all the wonderful experiences her years abroad were about to bring to her. I acknowledged that it would be different, and I would miss both my daughters a lot, but it would also allow me to focus on self-love and nurture. Our ephemeral separation was going to help all of us to grow.

Four women (my two daughters, my sister and I) were about to write the next chapter of our lives. I knew I would write this new chapter from a place where I would take charge and responsibility for my feelings and my emotions. If I don't like the way I feel, I know my perspective on the current situation can change in a moment. When I understood that, my life became so much simpler.

The Power of Unlearning

George Halfin

*'The first problem for all of us, men and women,
is not to learn, but to unlearn' – Gloria Steinem (1971)*

W hen I was in my twenties my mum always used to say to me 'George, why is your life so complicated?' – and to me it was. When I reflect on it now, I see that it was because I was always so desperate to do the 'right' thing and to please everyone so I would do things like dutifully go to all sorts of social events even if I didn't feel like it. I had no trust in myself, to the degree that I would ask everyone's advice on everything until my own small voice was often drowned out and I would be at a loss for what to do.

Life, especially work life, felt like a struggle because I was so desperate to control every aspect of it and not make any mistakes. I had this child-like fear of 'getting in trouble' and the belief that I had to be a 'good girl' all the time and I innocently and subconsciously took that very seriously. This affected both my work and social life.

I came out of university after studying business, thinking I could do anything. I managed to get an internship at a branding design agency which, thanks to me using my own initiative, led to a paid contract. I loved it there because you could truly be yourself and people valued that. Unfortunately, they couldn't keep me on, so I found a job as an account manager in a more established graphic design agency. The agency was going through a transition from its founders to a new set of directors, and my director was a complete workaholic and in retrospect, a bit of a control freak. (Put it this way: in a time before the internet, he threw the Yellow Pages* away because he thought it looked messy in the reception area.) He would leave Post-it notes all over my work to the degree that I lost confidence in my writing ability which haunted me for many years and fuelled my overthinking.

After a much-needed year off travelling, thanks to heeding the wisdom of my small voice, I went to work for another agency that specialised in marketing communications and events. I had many bosses in the two years I worked there, and the agency went through many changes. I kept my job until I was the last account manager standing before they closed, but during that time my fears and anxieties about making mistakes and things going wrong came back and internally grew and grew. I worked so hard and for such long hours that the stress gave me thrush because I wasn't looking after myself. I remember a colleague saying to me: 'George you always do a good job, but you don't look like you are enjoying it, and you always look so relieved when an event you have worked on is over.' That was very true. I would try to plan for every eventuality and cross every 't' and dot every 'i'. Yet for every event I was organising something would

---

*The Yellow Pages is a business telephone directory which was a big book used in the UK until the internet took over.

always go wrong that I hadn't planned for, and I would always find a way to deal with it, so that it worked out well in the end. Except I couldn't see that I had that ability, nor could I trust the process. To me the harder you worked the less things went wrong. Work was a stressful struggle!

I got burnt out and ended up working for my mum for a few years before returning to the workplace where I found what I perceived to be a less stressful job in a charity where they valued a work–life balance. During this time, outside of work, I made a documentary about dating and relationships and co-chaired a summer festival managing 60 volunteers to put on a three-day event for 600 people. I did all of this with ease and without the angst I felt in the workplace.

Roll on a few years and I found myself taking a job that my intellect told me to take because of the promotion and the money but my heart was screaming 'No!!!' It was working for some extremely successful people who I perceived in my head to be quite frightening, and I lived in fear of losing my job. This fed on my insecurities.

After I left this role, my cousin's wife was working for a charity that needed someone to organise their first wellbeing conference, so I took the job and did it as I did everything in work back then, taking it all very, very seriously. I felt very responsible for everything – to the extent that one day when the chairs were being delivered, I decided I couldn't disturb my colleagues as they were in a meeting. I would deal with it myself! This resulted in me running into a glass door, smashing my face in and welcoming everyone to the wellbeing conference with two black eyes! Even though I was running around being busy, I did manage to catch a few bits of the conference here and there and I could see how it was really impacting people. After the conference my boss kept me on and sent me to America to see this approach taught in probation centres, homeless shelters, and to kids whose behaviour meant they couldn't be in mainstream school. I was also lucky enough to get one-to-one coaching for a few days.

I came back and helped run their wellbeing programmes and sat in on the weekly women's group, but even though I could see other people getting something from it, I still couldn't work it out or understand it. My intellect was working on overdrive. Then one day I was on a bus and I started to feel anxious about something like, 'Did I lock the door?' I realised I was tired and maybe I was just anxious because I was tired, and it dropped away just like that. That sparked off a gradual unlearning that worked on me rather than me working on it that has carried on to this day. I noticed more and more situations in my day-to-day life where I wasn't so caught up in my thinking and was able to be more effective. I found myself less het up when cooking big family meals and even started enjoying the process rather than feeling so uptight that I would swear my head off in the kitchen. Small wins, but significant at the same time.

After a few years of seeing the benefits for myself, I decided I didn't want to just organise the wellbeing sessions. I wanted to learn to become a wellbeing teacher, so that is what I did. In one of my one-to-one sessions while I was doing my training, the course leader said to me 'I couldn't work with you, you're too intense.' I got really offended and upset and started crying. He felt terrible because he thought I knew, and I didn't. I genuinely didn't realise the extent to which I took my thinking so seriously and overthought everything. I remember one day soon after, sitting in the office feeling very overwhelmed by the amount of work I had to do and thinking it over and over in my head until, in a moment of insight that brought me to my senses, I realised 'I'm not doing any work; I'm just thinking about it!' How easy it is for thinking to take over and fuel more and more thinking if we take it seriously, believe it's worthy of attention and innocently fuel it.

I started to recognise that the uncomfortable feelings I experienced were almost always a signal that I wasn't in a good state of mind and taking life too seriously for whatever habitual reason, rather than something actually being wrong. When I was able to recognise this, which sometimes took longer than others, the feelings dropped away by themselves.

Once I started to more regularly notice where my thinking got in the way and gradually began to take it less seriously, my field of vision began to grow and grow and I began to trust myself and get comfortable in the unknown.

This has led me to flourish in my career in the last six years. After years of playing small, holding myself back and not being able to switch off from my work, I find myself navigating the ins and outs of work with a lot more ease and a lot less angst. Now reporting to director level at a national charity, I manage a diverse range of projects – often stepping into the unknown and feeling my way as I work on them. I love doing that now, whereas before the unknown was a place you didn't go because it was scary and uncontrollable. Now I take one step at a time doing what occurs to me to do and trusting it will work out as it should. I'm not saying I don't plan, I just plan with an open mind knowing that everything will take its course and whatever happens I will know what to do in the moment.

It's funny – I could look back and think about all those years I wasted holding myself back and being my own worst enemy and how it led to a very tumultuous career with many redundancies and other unpleasant situations. To some degree that's true but what's also true is that I wouldn't be doing what I'm doing today without those experiences.

What I've seen over the last eleven years and continue to see is the value of unlearning habits of thinking that innocently get in the way of us being all we can be in the world. If you are caught up in your thinking, you can't see all the options that are available. So, let's start to value unlearning as much as learning because both have their place.

Binning My 'Best Mum' Policy

Farah Halabi

Have I told you how I'm the perfect mum, with a perfect husband, a perfect home and perfect kids who don't fight with each other, don't talk back, are impeccably polite and worship the ground I walk on?

No?

Would you believe me if I told you how my life is like a never-ending Disney movie of angelic kids, laughter, fun, no arguments, NO computer games, which I just want to go on forever and how I dread my darlings going to school because I would just miss them too much?

Nope, neither would I, because unless I've just swallowed the blue pill and I'm still plugged into the Matrix, my reality up until now couldn't be more different... Think drama rather than Disney and instead of melodic, music-to-your-ears laughter, think high-pitched I'd-rather-burst-my-own-eardrums-than-listen-to-this-racket!

No one told me how hard this parenting gig is, or if they did I didn't believe them or I didn't hear because I was too caught up in setting in stone the rules and policies that would dictate what kind of parent I would be. I can laugh about it now, but when my firstborn made his debut, I distinctly remember promising God that I was going to be the best mum in the world. Of course, in turn, I vowed on my newborn's behalf that he was going to be the best, most amazing child in the history of children, ever.

Now, what that 'best mum' mirage looked like, I hadn't got the faintest idea but, in my head, it was like an enactment of the cheesiest Hallmark card, with a dash of hijabed Stepford Wives and the Waltons.

The way I showed up as a mum, in reality, was nothing short of a spectacular and monumental failure! I guess I could blame it on naivety but I'm a seasoned veteran mum of four kids. Quantity in this scenario really does not beget quality. Practice, it seems, does not make perfect. I was pretty good at being an equally awful mum to each of my kids. No favourites, just plain, good, old-fashioned sharing and doling out equal percentages of some really questionable parenting.

Monumental failure was a term not solely reserved for my mothering skills (or lack thereof). It appeared that being the best mum in the world required much more than all the energy I had which left nothing for my husband, my home or even myself. My cup was empty, but furthermore, it was chipped, cracked and leaking!

Something had to give and so hubby was sentenced to Room 101, the drawer in the filing cabinet in my mind labelled 'later', as too was my self-care. I had convinced myself that in order to fulfil my self-imposed policy of being the best mum in the world, I needed to focus every atom of my very being on the kids and nothing but the kids. Once I'd cracked that, then and only then would I be able to begin to be a better mum and after that maybe a good wife.

Boy, how wrong was I? After summers of meticulously planning my children's 'break' with military-style precision, organising, diarising playdate after football/karate camp, swimming, extended family visits, baking days and reluctant computer console sessions, it finally hit me, like a crazy epiphany... my kids were miserable. Instead of the amazing behaviour and happiness I had expected my efforts to produce, I was met with temper tantrums, fighting, rudeness and complete exhaustion which I mistakenly read as ingratitude. The more their behaviour was off track, the more I disliked them. If I was a monumental failure before, now I was hands down the worst mum in the history of mothers, ever, in the universe.

My life truly and irrevocably changed when my search for a better way, a saner way to parent, led me down the path of self-awareness, to discover how a simple shift in my thinking would reveal the truth that has ultimately set me free and restored the blessings and peace in my home.

Now... I actually enjoy spending time with all my children, together at home, and I can relax.

Believe me when I tell you that this was a total game changer for me. 'Kids' and 'relax' were two words I never ever thought I'd say in the same sentence. I love my children, but somehow that didn't translate into enjoying their company or feeling like I was good enough for them to want to spend time with me. I truly believed that I couldn't relax or feel any semblance of peace unless my kids were away from me. Now I see that my kids are not the source of my stress, and that my peace is inside of me and not dependent on what goes on outside of me.

Now... I don't plan as much and I consult rather than dictate.

It's my way or the highway! I actually loved this saying. Not only was this an acceptable concept but it was the most obvious because what other way was there? How I showed up as a mum changed when I realised that the map of parenting I had drawn in my head was not set in stone. Any decent sat-nav will show you more than one way or reroute you if you take a wrong turn. All roads lead to Rome, but I could only see one way and I was convinced that I could predict and foretell the outcome of any parenting situation. This rendered the involvement of anyone else, in any decision-making, obsolete. I realised that if I wanted my children to thrive, the foundation from which I parented had to change, and my baseline shifted from authoritative to under-standing and inclusiveness. I now accept that my map may not be the one I initially planned out but it can be one that is right for us in this moment. We certainly haven't transformed into a perfect, trouble-free family, but in partnering up with my kids, connecting with rather than correcting them, difficult moments rarely become full-on dramas and the onus is on progression rather than perfection.

Now... I see past their behaviour. I see my kids for who they are.

I don't do labels, or so I thought, but I realised I was guilty of only ever seeing my kids in terms of their behaviour... moody, diffi-cult, obstinate, boisterous or defiant. Being able to look beneath the surface of their behaviour allowed me to understand their big emotions like anger, frustration, disappointment and anxiety, and to deal with what's really going on. Through the simple mindset shift, I understood that I was not actually dealing with an [insert label] child but instead saw that I can only ever experience my child through my own state of mind. That insightful understanding completely flips everything about how I parent on its head. Our children are more than just their behaviours and personalities – and it is only by seeing past this that we can see who they really are and bring out the best in them.

In previous years, even the thought of the holidays and being together with my children, filled me with dread. The experience was quite simply awful. The way things look now from the outside isn't so drastically different but *my experience*, the way *I feel* and *think* about it, is different, and it's the inside that has monumentally and amazingly transformed... that's where the magic's happened.

My inner suffering and conflict were dispelled, leaving space for peaceful, deep, harmonious connection with everyone, my children, my husband, myself and God. I now enjoy my life with my children instead of feeling like I'm treading water and just about surviving.

Parenting my four cherubs is largely based on refereeing and crowd control. I couldn't understand why my children didn't listen to me the first time I'd ask, or why they argued with each other over nothing. All I saw was their off-track behaviour. Coercion and threats only yielded compliance, not cooperation. By zooming out and giving them space to access their own innate wisdom, they were able to find their own solutions.

Shouting at my kids was never going to be conducive to them behaving better, and I realised that wasn't even why I was doing it, even though I thought it was. Shouting was for me, to prove how angry I was, to vent my own frustration, to release the pent-up anguish that my kids wouldn't just do what I said at the time I said it. When I insightfully saw that they were not the source of my feelings and they couldn't 'make' me shout, the penny dropped. I only ever shout if my mind is busy at the time. My thinking in any given moment is what causes my feelings. If I have a quiet mind, the way in which I respond to my children's off-track behaviour is more peaceful and calm. If my mind is busy... then take cover, it's every kid for themselves.

Now... I have binned my 'best mum' policy and given myself a break.

My parenting and everyday life (in my head) used to look like the Tasmanian Devil. I had set the highest, most unrealistic expectations of what being a good mum, a perfect mum, meant, and every day was a smack in the face, reminding me what a failure I was. I was exhausted from constantly worrying about what people thought of me as a mum because I had shackled my self-worth and purpose in life to the role of motherhood. Therefore, my mothering had to be Oscar-worthy. I just didn't feel good enough. This notion permeated through all my anxieties and fears. It was a constant mantra, the tiny voice in my head confirming my 'worst mum' status every time I messed up with my kids.

The most fundamental transformation came when I realised that the story I was telling myself wasn't true. I had planted the belief that I wasn't good enough at my baseline and worked everything up from there to give substance and evidence to support it. I had the insight that I was not created unworthy or not good enough. The way I perceived myself was all made up. I had unconsciously bought into the illusion that my thoughts were concrete and could give weight and substance to define me. I've been shown the true nature and source of my thoughts and feelings; they come and even if they stick around for a bit, they will go. It is only when I attach meaning and importance to them that they can appear to be more than what they really are. When all thoughts are stripped away, what's left is what I really am... not a mum, sister, wife, daughter or even Farah, that's just a name. I am a soul; I am enough, because I am.

From this baseline, I am grateful to The One who created me. I give gratitude for the many blessings in my life: children to clean up after, a home to share their laughter in, a husband to share my joys with, and the power of thought that allows me to navigate and experience these blessings. From a place of inner peace and clarity, I can see my 'best mum' policy is completely fictitious and so there is no need to live up to it. My purpose and self-worth are not measured by my parenting but that's not to say I shouldn't try my best... I just know that there is no 'best' version, there's just me and that's perfect!

The Small Shaft of Light

Angela Dawson

This is *my life*, I thought, as I lay on my back on the floor beside the bathroom door on the upstairs landing. My left arm is hooked over Larry, who, despite giggling and sort-of singing along to a song I'd made up only moments earlier, is now snuffling, soft and steady. What I'd assumed were joke snores, turned out to be the real thing. Amidst all the noise, somehow, my son has fallen asleep. So here I am. Trapped.

How did I get here?

The first time I saw him, I wondered how his legs would ever hold him. Growing small in the last two weeks, he turned out to be the biggest of all my babies. It was past eleven at night. Minutes before, I'd moved my swollen, naked body from the centre of the pool over to my husband. 'I'm really sorry. I have to get out,' I'd said, in a muffled, mumbled voice that seemed far away from me. Birthing has a way of taking you over and out of yourself, if you let it.

I know it's going to be soon... I just... don't know what to do with myself.

We held each other, kissed, me softening into his strength. In the half-light, he helped me step over the edge and onto the stool. Two steps later, I was down. As soon as my feet touched the ground, I knew I had to get back in. I needed the water.

Arching high. Growling low.

The midwife wiped her glasses, thinking there were a few spare minutes. My son had other ideas. In four short moves, he was out, bursting through the water with his life-rope secure.

Did I reach for him, or was he passed to me? I can't recall. All I remember is, once he was of my body, then he was on it, all wrinkled and puffed and soft-skinned.

I leant back against the side of the pool. Took him in.

The tops of his feet, first pressed against his thin shins, flapped forwards like a cartoon duck. *How will you ever stand, son?*

His almond eyes were dark and deep. I lost myself in them, thought he was a wise one from another world. In a flash, the classic alien face popped to mind. Larry looked like this. Almost black upturned eyes. Big forehead. Tiny chin. This boy of mine. He was a wonder.

And now, almost four years later, here we are. Wedged between the cold, hard wall and the bathroom door, in a space as wide as my son is tall.

A sharp draught curls its way under the gap, where the door and the floor don't quite meet. It hits me square on my right shoulder. The hairs on my skin prick up in a desperate bid to trap a bit of warmth. I shiver. Wonder again, 'How did I get here?' A summer-born girl with more than a drop of Caribbean blood, I am no big fan of the cold. At our annual home-ed camp, I go to bed in multiple layers. Vest. Long-sleeve top. Ankle-length nightie. Thin jumper. Hoodie. Plus socks. And pyjama bottoms. My husband wears a single T-shirt and a pair of knee-length shorts. So, no. I am not a fan of the cold.

I sigh as fully as I can without disturbing Larry. I may be irked at my ridiculous predicament, but I am no fool. I know it's best to let sleeping babes lie.

Maybe I can inch-worm my way over to Maisie's room. My daughter loves soft furnishings. She has piles of blankets and pillows and cushions all jumbled up on her bed. If only I could get them, Larry could be safe and warm and I could be getting on with the multitude of things a mother-writer can be getting on with when she has unexpected free time: drying dishes, drafting stories, daydreaming.

But there's no easy way to safely extricate myself without exposing him to the potential perils my overactive imagination has conjured. Pictures of him smashing his head against the wall as he turns in his sleep. Or plummeting down the stairs. My mind gives me no rest. So, for now, I am here to stay.

I stare into space, contemplating my fate. As I lose myself, I notice the small shaft of light that creeps under the bathroom door along with the chill. Something inside me begins to soften.

Straight ahead, is my daughter's door, with the decoupaged denim 'M' and the handmade sign. The cold wall on my left is home to the double-backed bunting she made in her first sewing machine class some years back when she was eight. Triangles of stars and flowers and birds and fake dalmatian fur are slung over the ballet barre-style banister. A local graffiti artist's 'Ship Shape and Bristol Fashion' print hangs above. It reminds me of my husband's fortieth and the nearby neighbourhood we lived in for almost a decade. My eldest son's room is behind my head.

All around, my past meets my present.

My mind travelled far and wide in those few short minutes.

It remembered the girl in primary school who'd given all her classmates a pocket-sized British Sign Language alphabet card. Twenty-six small squares of tiny hands shaping letters. How this talking with hands became a helpful skill with my firstborn, essential for my last.

It remembered the slim Pelican book with the red circle on the cover. How this chance encounter in a charity shop set me on this child-led learning path before any of my children were inklings.

I looked up at the ceiling and some words came drifting back to me.

As I remember it, the magic-making man told of how, every day, people the world over dream of different ways of living and being. Thousands upon thousands of times, over the course of a life. It stands to reason that, at some point in time, someone, somewhere, will dream of living a life that looks like mine.

An ordinary existence. One of domesticity. Of raising young souls and letting them become. A slow lane life, filled with odd moments of harmony.

Yes, this is my life. Lying with arms wrapped around warm flesh; feeling the spirit of my family wrapped around me. The annoyance slowly fades. Who's to say lying on the landing with a sleeping tot isn't important work?

This is *my* life.

In this moment I claim it. For now, at least, the disparate strands seem to stitch together. The steps I've taken make some kind of sense.

Surrounded by these threads of my past which have led to this moment, I know it could be no other way.

A slow grin spreads over my face as I imagine sharing what I 'do' for a living with the now-grown girls of my old Catholic comprehensive. I wonder at the curious contentment I feel in being a midlife mother. Trapped and chilled at the top of the stairs, wanting for all the world, no other life.

A muffled chuckle bubbles up at this unexpected insight.

Though still physically stuck, my mind and spirit are free.

In this quiet space of surrender and acceptance, a new plan hatches. I whisper it into Larry's ear.

I hitch him over my chest and belly, cradle him in the crook of my right arm, grab the banister with my left hand. In one graceless arc, I am half-up, sitting on the floor. I bum-shuffle my way to the top of the stairs, then stand, softly speaking in his ear all the while. I carry him down, shielding his eyes from the sunshine.

He fidgets a little as I lie him on his floor-bed, eyes crinkling at the brightness. Somehow, he stays asleep. I close the curtains and let him be.

Finding Peace in Impossible Circumstances

Debra Simmons

As I write this, my son is twenty-three years old.

He is alive and well and is one of the most amazing, inspiring young men I know. I'm very proud of him.

When Josh was born, I was in a very unhealthy relationship with his dad.

Josh didn't have the best start in life.

He learned about manipulation, aggression, insecurity and fear.

He grew up witnessing the worst of humanity.

I was afraid and on tenterhooks much too often to be a good mum to him.

He struggled as a kid, even as a baby he wasn't happy.

My husband and I split up when he was a nine-year-old hurt, angry and confused little boy. He grew into a teenager with attitude and issues.

The good news about those years, as he grew up, was that I was learning things about how life works and myself and becoming a better person, and a better parent.

I could see how I had gotten myself into the mess that I had been in.

I could see why my now ex-husband had done the things he had done.

I could see that blame and judgment made things worse, not better.

I could see why my son was struggling and suffering like he was.

I knew that underneath all the struggling and suffering there was something about my son that could never be damaged or broken.

I knew that me realising this about both of us, was having a positive effect on him and that if he were to see it for himself then his life would become much easier, as mine had.

I just didn't know if I was ever going to share what I knew with him.

Until out of the blue, one ordinary summer evening when Josh was twenty-one this happened...

I needed to go out to collect a travel cot for my daughter's baby boy, it was about an hour's drive away.

Josh asked to join me.

I was surprised. It wasn't like him, but of course, I said yes.

We jumped into my dark blue Skoda Fabia.

As we were fastening our seat belts, Josh rubbed his fingers along the dust on the dashboard and laughed.

'Mum, you really need to clean this car.'

I always kept my car free of clutter and rubbish, but he was right it was thick with dust and needed a good clean.

I laughed too and gently punched his upper arm. He was broad and muscley and had a tattoo that made his arm look as if it were robotic.

'You could help me out and do it for me.'

I looked at him as I spoke, his eyes had dark circles underneath them and the whites were pinker than white. His face was pale, the thought that something wasn't right crossed my mind.

I didn't say anything.

I pressed the start button and put the car into gear, focusing on my neighbour's driveway as I manoeuvred out onto the road.

The conversation flowed freely between us, as I drove.

We reached our destination and picked up the cot.

As I got back into the car, Josh looked at me and took a breath.

'Mum, I need to talk to you.'

He was shifting in his seat, struggling with the words.

I restarted the car and said, 'OK – I'm listening.'

Josh looked at me, he had tears in his eyes as he spoke, his voice breaking a little,

'Mum I can't do life anymore,' he paused and took another breath. 'It's just too hard,' he said on the slow outbreath.

I felt as if I had been punched in the stomach.

I was thrown off guard for a minute, the conversation earlier hadn't prepared me for this. Not right now, I wasn't ready. I would never be ready.

It was my turn to take a breath.

'What do you mean?' I asked, too quickly, then slightly more slowly, 'Tell me what that means.'

'I think you know.'

He was looking down at his hands in his lap as he spoke.

I thought I knew, I didn't want to know, it was too painful.

My head was going crazy.

Then almost unnoticed the thought that my peripheral vision was impressive crossed my mind, followed by, how can you be thinking something so unimportant now?

As I saw those thoughts cross my mind the spell of the moment broke. I can only describe it like this, it seemed as if I fell out of the fear and back into what I knew about life.

What I had been learning and personally experiencing.

There was more available than just the circumstances that were playing out.

I had noticed thought doing what thought does, passing through my mind, bringing a feeling with it.

I knew this wasn't the first time Josh had struggled to the extent that he wanted to take his life.

It had been very difficult as a mum to watch him go to such dark places and to suffer so painfully. But in that moment, strange as it seemed, as I saw through my thinking, I was at peace. I knew he was ok no matter what he was feeling and that this was the best way he knew how to deal with what was going on for him.

I knew I was OK too, no matter what the outcome.

That felt both surprising and comforting, it gave me clarity and peace, the ability to be part of the solution, not part of the problem.

I felt so much compassion, I could feel it as if it was a physical thing.

I had no desire to make Josh do anything he didn't want to.

I knew instinctively that wouldn't help.

It would be what I wanted, against what he wanted.

It wouldn't be love and acceptance of each other, it would be more busy craziness for us both.

I wanted for him what he wanted for himself.

If that was to take his own life, then even that was OK.

I wanted to listen to him without judgment or fear.

It was my turn to take a breath.

'Let's have a different conversation about this,' I spoke softly.

'First I want to say thank you for sharing this with me, it can't have been easy.' There were tears rolling down my cheeks and the love I was feeling for this beautiful human being next to me was immense.

'Josh, I love you way too much to tell you what to do or that you should be different, or you shouldn't think or feel the way you do.'

I took a breath and wiped the tears so I could see to drive.

'Could I just share something that's really helped me?'

All the time I was speaking, I was watching the road unfold in front of me and marvelling at the ordinariness of the day, sheep grazing in the field, a tarmac road, a blue car, a dull evening sky.

I was watching my thoughts too.

I was aware of the incredible peace that was available amid such potential devastation.

I clicked the indicator as I came to a turning, and glanced at Josh looking for confirmation to continue.

He nodded.

'We live every moment in the feeling of what we think. We don't feel our circumstances or what appears to be going on around us, we feel what we're thinking in that second and as our thoughts change our experience changes.

'I know you feel shitty and desperate right now, I know you want that feeling to go away, I would too.

'I also think that just saying out loud that you want to end your life brings some sort of relief, changes the feeling a little bit.'

His head moved slightly in confirmation.

'I know you think there's something wrong with you, because you feel so bad. I know you feel trapped, but strange as it seems that thought of suicide is your wisdom, your inner guidance, giving you a taste of the relief that's on offer here.

'The only thing *wrong* is that you're misunderstanding how you work and your own self-righting system.

'You work perfectly, but nobody's shown you the instructions.

'Once you see them, you won't feel this way anymore, understanding yourself will give you even more relief.'

I paused; the fields had changed into houses as we drove into the town.

There was a layby at the side of the road, I pulled in and turned to face Josh.

'I love you whatever you do, you don't have to be here for me to love you, I would prefer you were here, but my love doesn't depend on it.'

I stopped speaking as we both cried.

I don't know how long we sat there, but eventually Josh broke the silence.

'Thanks Mum, my head feels like it's gonna explode with everything in it.

'I'm scared to let it out.

'I know it's gotta come out. It won't stay inside anymore.

'I'm scared of life, not death, life.

'My thoughts scare me, I want to bash my own head into smithereens, I don't know what to do with everything in my head.

'I need killing myself as an option, I can't let it go, I just can't!'

He cried out from all the pain he was carrying, his huge shoulders heaving up and down as the sobs let go into a wail and he cried and cried.

Something changed for Josh on that day.

It took a while, but this conversation was the start of some amazing exchanges between us, conversations that are still ongoing. I no longer teach Josh anything, he teaches me. Or perhaps we learn together.

He is interested in how his thoughts impact his mental health and what's possible no matter what he's thinking.

This is the tip of a conversational iceberg that is bigger and more impactful than the one that sank the *Titanic*.

I am eternally grateful that it is a conversation I'm a part of.

It brings me immense peace, joy and fun and gives me what I need even in the most impossible of circumstances.

It is in the words of a good friend of mine, both profoundly practical and practically profound.

Coming Home to Joy and Peace

Sue Pankiewicz

I write this at the age of sixty-four. I have a wonderful husband, four adult children, four beautiful grandchildren, a delightful dog and a comfortable home in a rural village that I love. I have a vivid sense of the beauty and perfection that surrounds me: I feel at home in my home and in myself, for enough of the time, to have immense gratitude. I know what peace of mind is and I take things seriously only when it makes sense to do so, generally living in a lighter and more relaxed frame of mind.

Prior to this, I was serious about so much for more than forty years! Being serious seemed natural, almost inevitable, as there was always a lot to consider, to make better or improve. I don't see it as a decision I took but rather a reaction to what I made of life. Light-hearted moments, laughter and fun were present but experienced more as interruptions to the serious preoccupations of managing life as a child in my family home and later as an adult in my own home. Surprisingly, no one appeared to notice, or ever asked when I was growing up, if I was happy or felt secure. Maybe it was because those sorts of conversations were rare in those days. This also might have been due to the fact that

I became an expert at hiding my feelings, separating my inside from my outside, adapting my behaviours to survive the turmoil and uncertainty of a bitterly unhappy home. Ironically, our family would have looked fine to the outside world even though, at its heart, it was so often a desperately unhappy place.

Keeping up appearances was confusing and I believe it laid the foundations for what was normal and shaped how I continued to live. Running away at seventeen was my way of leaving home. I couldn't imagine how my parents would fare without me as a go-between and, as a result, I had carried a strong feeling of responsibility towards them.

I lived into adulthood with an increasing sense that something was not right, that something was missing. I would sum it up now as the gap between how I felt as 'me' and the 'happiness' I craved. This lack was serious to me. I recognised the disconnect between how I felt a lot of the time and how I behaved. I wanted so much to have a happy marriage. I didn't want to recreate what I had seen in my parents' relationship, but I didn't know how to achieve it. I am grateful that in my professional life and in my friendships, I experienced a more authentic version of myself.

Ever in search of answers, solutions and fixes, I spent many years as a seeker of self-help aids. During the early years of marriage and following the advent of motherhood I was consumed with trying to figure out how to create the happiness I longed for.

Becoming a parent added to the already-present pressure of what I see now as deep-rooted feelings of insecurity, along with an inner sense of lostness that at the time created such loneliness despite being surrounded by family and friends. I embarked on my first pregnancy with such powerful intentions. I would be a modern 'earth mother', with babies so beautifully nurtured they would never need to cry. I would breastfeed without schedule and make full use of a sling to keep them close. Oh, the fun I would have with this firstborn, this new little being. Hypnobirthing was prepared for with such confidence and optimism and surely this would be the start of becoming the real me – an absolute success story called, 'Motherhood – creating the happy family'.

I see now that after giving birth for the first time I was mentally and emotionally derailed. I had failed both with hypnobirthing and a drug-free labour and fairly rapidly became sleep-deprived and anxious. Three weeks previously I had been at work, full of optimism, and suddenly I was at home alone with a baby who cried a great deal and woke every two hours through the night. I felt desperate but unable to express it, needed help and support and didn't know how to ask for it.

With the arrival of two more children, I was now overwhelmed with a sense of the 'gap' – between the vision I carried within me of what a family should be like, what a marriage should be like, how much happiness, fun and joy we should all experience, and the very different reality that I perceived existed. Everything felt serious and effortful as I analysed, intellectualised and strived to attain the standards I imagined I should achieve. My mind was consumed with thoughts of how to work it all out, how to solve the problem of failing in so many areas – and all the while you would never have guessed! I could make people laugh, I could arrange elaborate children's birthday parties, the house was open to the children's friends, and we had the appearance of having a great family life.

Fast-forward through a traumatic experience of divorce, children who now included a stepdaughter, who each coped very differently and none of whom escaped, with even our best attempts to save them, from fear, anxiety and hurt. The guilt of this was exhausting. I tried so hard to compensate for the break-up of our family, which was in my mind an appalling failure to provide a stable, happy home which I had been trying to create for so many years.

When my second daughter had a psychotic breakdown at seventeen during her first year of A-levels, I was thrown into fear, panic and relentless guilt. The signs of her unhappiness had been there; I should have been more aware, but I had no idea how to deal with a gradually worsening situation. Her succession of mixed-up, wayward school friends, a situation at school where a computer technician was discovered making initial attempts to groom her, an attachment to an older boyfriend which enabled time away from home and, as it turned out, a dive into drug-taking. My feelings of guilt went to the core of my being. My lovely girl, who should have been enjoying a fun-filled arrival into adulthood as per my blueprint, was by the age of eighteen diagnosed with schizophrenia with full-blown symptoms including hearing voices and paranoia.

The impact was huge on our other children as we attempted to shield them whilst our lives became consumed within a new world of mental health services. My second marriage was to the most wonderfully grounded man I think I have ever known. I will always be grateful for his support even as, at the time, I included him in the line-up of who was in some way responsible and to blame. I had pole position of course for being the absolute worst failure as a mother. It was an unbearable, frantic, panicked and frightening period of my life.

I don't know if anyone is ever prepared to enter a psychiatric ward to visit their beautiful daughter who has been sectioned. I felt helpless, inadequate, sidelined by the system, strung out with such anxiety that I could barely function. And yet, somehow, I went through the motions of living and attending to basic functions. I was a senior schoolteacher and was granted compassionate leave, for which I will always be so grateful as I loved my schoolwork – the place where I seemed to fit into the outline of my imagined self – a successful, happy and popular professional. Ironically, although I was entirely conscientious, hard-working, enjoyed my pupils and the rapport in my classrooms, my work carried none of the heavy-weighted feeling of seriousness that permeated the rest of my life experience. Somehow this person was left behind on the journey home each day.

During the following years, my daughter attempted suicide at least twice with additional sectionings. Thankfully, I began to gain an understanding of the tortuous life I had innocently created for myself, including the crushing feelings of responsibility for failing my child. As a bright but extremely insecure child, growing up in a dysfunctional family, I had emerged as an adolescent with well-practised emotional coping strategies for covering up fears, tactics to conceal my inner turmoil, and a detachment to protect me – none of which I realised at the time and all of which I believe was experienced by my own children. To a large extent I was emotionally unavailable to my children and carried feelings of inadequacy on top of that ongoing quest to find happiness. These two examples illustrate this:

- I remember being in the kitchen, preoccupied with a situation that had arisen between my first husband and I, whilst my elder daughter stood by my side talking to me. I was aware she was speaking, because I could see her, but I realised I couldn't actually hear her, such was the noise in my head. She was just four at the time. I was shocked into recognition that I just wasn't there – the outside of me was but the inside of me was not. I had stood in her shoes as a child myself and knew the loneliness of having an absent-minded mother and yet here I was seemingly unable to be different despite all my efforts.

- My father died suddenly of a massive heart attack on the eve of my elder daughter's fifth birthday party. Thirty children were expected, a magic clown entertainer had been booked and I had yet to finish her clown-shaped cake. I managed superbly well and despite the head of the clown rolling off at 3 a.m., I fixed it. I welcomed children and parents as though all was well. In an odd way I think it was just a more extreme version of my ability to switch off on the inside whilst performing on the outside. I might have been a million miles away in my mind, but I could still appear as the serenely competent mother. It was as if I was continually proving to others that I was fine, for fear of exposing the mess inside.

I continued to research alternative therapies, fixated on finding a cure for my own 'out of sorts' state of mind whilst my love, understanding and compassion for my ill daughter was contaminated with fearful, unrelenting thought streams, anxiety and exhaustion. The result was ongoing, flailing attempts to fix the 'problem'. I couldn't understand why this showed up in my behaviour as frustration, criticism, bullying and intolerance when I was with her. I was devoted to her wellbeing but of course still felt like I was failing as she didn't magically heal and reappear as the daughter I lost. I'd arrive to visit and there would be a reality shock – her unkempt appearance preoccupied me, her bleached hair upset me, her disorganised and at times delusional, sped-up thoughts and speech patterns distressed me. I'd try to conceal my feelings and often left hiding a flood of tears and distress.

Some years into this ongoing crisis, I was exposed to a powerful explanation that surpassed everything else I had ever learned and made sense of every experience I had ever had, or indeed would have, in the future. So powerful was this that I left my teaching career to share what I had learned, as a mentor, facilitator and teacher. As a result of this I slowly emerged from the weight of my own serious, fearful and unhelpful habitual thinking and began to see something I had previously been blinded to. I saw that everyone has their own innate wealth of mental health, their own wisdom, their own capacity to heal. When I began to understand that, I began to see more of it appearing – I saw what was always whole, undamaged and well, existed for my daughter and in me.

My daughter is married to the original 'older boyfriend' and they have now been together for over twenty years. Yes, she hears voices; yes, she is still on anti-psychotic medication; yes, she is still running a bit fast; and yes, I find her ebullience hard to cope with sometimes – but none of that seems so out of the ordinary or so serious now. I can mostly regard it as quirks of behaviour as opposed to signs of mental illness, so it doesn't add up to a serious concern or a problem. They face challenges together with great resilience and the support we offer is mainly practical. I can now disregard fears for their future, regrets from the past and any sense of the need to make things better as simply thoughts that come and go.

Moreover, I can see my daughter's acceptance of my behaviours towards her – which were generated through my fears, impatience, intolerances, lack of understanding and desire to fix – has actually served as a guide. She has shown me unconditional love and regard, never uttering a critical remark, aptly managing me with the gentlest skills – she could be a professional subject changer! Once I stopped being interested in and paying heed to my own inner fearful dialogue, I became more present and thus our relationship took on a lighter feel. I gained far more respect, admiration and trust in who she is, rather than who I thought I wanted her to be.

Seriousness once played a huge role in my life, showing up as the qualities of a conscientious, dedicated, responsible and caring person. Now I find I am serious when it serves me. It is no longer my default state of mind which unknown to me used to create the filter through which I saw life. My happiness and peace of mind arise without effort as a natural implication of no longer paying attention to, or believing in, the reliability or truth of fearful thoughts. When seriousness became redundant, I came home to me and a life of wonder and joy.

Learning to Live Beyond the Story

Kate Dalgliesh

I was invited to write this chapter a while ago and I realise I have been putting it off, held back by a thought: 'How can I put this understanding into words, without it being lost in translation?' Focusing on this one thought created my experience. I was taking it too seriously. I felt stuck.

Then, this morning out of the blue, an old friend from school got in touch; we haven't seen each other for thirty years. At the end of the conversation, she mentioned that her daughter is suffering with anxiety and refusing to go to school. I decided at that moment that I would leave my ego aside and share my story. My husband said, 'just write it from the heart, Kate', and I realise this is all I can do. I am pointing to something which ultimately people have been seeing and experiencing for themselves for centuries. A life less serious, with more joy and magic. Whether you hear or not will be down to you and your willingness to let go of everything you *thought* you knew.

'When you've exhausted all possibilities, remember this: you haven't...' – Thomas Edison (Schuller, 1984)

At the age of seventeen, I remember sitting in my friend Ella's Ford Fiesta, and her passing comment: 'Kate, do you know what your problem is? You take life too seriously!' If only I had known back then the wisdom in those words and what they were pointing towards.

I had not realised that I took life particularly seriously until my middle child, Georgia (aged 12 at the time), started to suffer with anxiety. Over the course of three years, she went from being a relaxed, happy, sporty school girl with lots of friends, to a fearful rabbit caught in the headlights. Eventually she refused to go to school altogether. I saw no choice but to engage seriously with Georgia's anxiety. What I didn't see was that, in buying into her story, I was innocently keeping it alive. My child was looking to me for love and guidance, and I wasn't able to give her the reassurance she was craving. It was as though she were whispering 'I don't feel OK, Mummy. Am I OK?' But I was too wrapped up in seriousness to hear her. I was so busy focusing on the behaviour, the anxiety, the 'sideshow', that I missed the main event – Georgia's unbreakable spirit, standing there right in front of me.

I started to search for solutions. As humans we can't seem to look at a problem and a solution at the same time. I had become fixated with the problem, the anxiety, and I had the very serious task of fixing my daughter. I would be a terrible mother if I didn't take this incredibly seriously. Georgia continued to feel my heaviness, my fear, my judgement. I thought I was showing love, but love is not born out of fear.

Back then I thought that life happened to us, outside in. I looked on the outside for answers. I blamed the impatient maths teacher, the tempestuous sports coach. I read the research on the highly sensitive child and immediately pinned this label to Georgia. I saw everything filtered through this belief. We were both innocently trapped in a story, stuck in the same chapter over and over, not seeing that we could turn the page. I dragged Georgia along to various counsellors and endless sessions of cognitive behavioural therapy. All well intentioned, but all looking at the behaviour, not the whole. Georgia dug her heels in and refused to engage. 'Why are you all trying to fix me? Do you *really* think I am broken?' It felt all wrong to her, but her pilot light never went out. 'Please keep looking, Mum!'

It was January 2019 when I finally came across the teachings of Sydney Banks, The Three Principles and Innate Health. We started to listen to a few online videos. I watched as Georgia's pilot light started to burn brighter. This was the first thing that made any sense to her. The relief was palpable, as I saw her get lost in a lovely feeling. Where was the anxiety now?

Focusing on the anxiety had made us both very heavy and closed-minded. We think that by being serious and looking more and more at the problem we will find the answer. Focus on the seriousness of the problem and that's all you see. You are stuck.

I began to listen more. Life does not happen to us, as we are encouraged to believe; life happens from within. We live in our individual thought-created realities. We live our stories. While something looks true to us, we experience it as true. While we are focusing on anxious thoughts, we are going to live in the experience of anxiety. As Michael Neill says, with this understanding we transform from being the frightened passenger at the back of the plane feeling all the turbulence, to becoming the pilot.

'Your thoughts are like the artist's brush. They create a personal *picture of the reality you live in.'* – Sydney Banks (1998)

It was now February and although we intellectually understood that Georgia was innocently engaging with anxious thinking and creating her reality, we hadn't really felt the depth of this understanding from within. We were listening using our intellects, using it as a tool to 'fix' Georgia. There was still an undercurrent of fear. Take life too seriously and you think you are keeping safe, but you miss the point.

'A ship is always safe at the shore but this is not what a ship was built for.' – Source disputed

My sister encouraged me to get more help, find another therapist specialising in children with anxiety. Instead, I called Jenny Elleray and her husband Dave. I took Georgia on a four-day retreat, still with the very serious intention of 'fixing' her. Dave and Jen, with their beautifully humble way of sharing The Three Principles behind life, reminded me that we are nature, created with the same perfection. The intelligence behind life doesn't make mistakes. My thinking calmed down, all my seriousness fell away and I began to feel from within the true essence of life. The truth of Georgia's unbreakable spirit. She was not broken, not lacking in any way. As the seriousness and fear melted away, so the illusion of separation evaporated, and I could see Georgia as though for the first time. The joy, the relief and light-heartedness flooded back in.

In allowing myself to sink more deeply into this understanding, I have found a space of reflection. I had previously thought that by taking life seriously I would find all the answers I needed. I have now seen the opposite to be true. When we let go of all our thinking and find that space within ourselves, beyond all personal thought, which some have called 'wisdom', we find the answers we are searching for. This wisdom is always there but for our thinking, in the same way the sun is always there but for the clouds. Focus on the clouds and that is all you see. Knowing that the sun is always there brings back the joy, magic and fun into life.

I started to see the different states of being serious and light-hearted. One being closed-minded, the other full of possibility and hope. Who told us to take life so seriously in the first place? We are not born serious after all. When we worry about our children, we innocently lose connection with them. When we get stuck in our seriousness, they hear judgement and criticism. That illusion of separation. We lose our common sense and feel out of control. Tune in to that inner space and we see the answers that were there all along *but* for our thinking. When we start to trust and tap into an intelligence far greater than our own limited thoughts, we can let go of the heaviness. Georgia's anxiety went from being a problem, to being a wonderful opportunity for growth. I can now take a step back and see my children's lives more impersonally with added respect for their own resilience. Whatever they go through, the foundations are always there. This is not to say I am detached or indifferent, it is in fact the polar opposite. Not bogged down with concern and worry, I see their innate wellbeing. This can never be broken. 'Is Mum worried about me?... No... OK, so I don't need to worry about me either...' The result: a life less serious.

Georgia is now back at school, has strong friendships, enjoys her passion for art and climbing, and no longer feels compelled to focus on anxious thoughts. On the occasions that she does engage with an insecure thought, and so create her experience, she is more willing to simply allow the anxiety to pass through her in the knowledge that it cannot hurt her. She knows it will pass. There are no right or wrong feelings; they are all manifestations of our thinking. The more we experience the truth of this, the more we feel it within and we realise there is nothing to fear.

'If the only thing people learned was not to be afraid of their experience, that alone would change the world.'
– Sydney Banks (1998)

Making Peace with Uncertainty

Christine Heath

I was the youngest of four children and was born during a time of great loss in my family. My fathers' parents both died in the first year of my life, his brother died the following year, his best friend and my godfather died the next year, and my father had a heart attack the year after that. He was given three years to live and we all knew that this was really serious! We all adored my father, who was a very gentle and loving man. It was earth-shattering to think that his days were limited. The fear of my father dying seemed very real to all of us, although no one talked about it, almost as if not talking about it would make it not happen. We all held our breath waiting for the day he would pass away, for over twenty years! I was always thinking about his death and how it would impact me and how sad it would make me. Life looked scary to me and it seemed as if there was so much I couldn't control.

It seemed as if uncertainty about the future would be the story of my life. In a paper I wrote in the ninth grade, I shared that I was afraid of being hurt by men even though I lived in a small town in Minnesota and we didn't even lock our doors. At this time, I didn't think that I was a serious person. I thought life was full of uncontrollable things that, if they happened, would be awful. In fact, at a class reunion, one of my best friends asked me why I had always been so serious in high school. I was very insecure, but had no idea that others could see it.

I struggled with negative thoughts about my body, my abilities, and my lovability throughout my college years and had lots of fears about life. Things happened which reinforced the perception I had that life was scary and bad things happened randomly. A burglar assaulted me and my roommate was raped while I was in college. That really made all my fears look valid and true. I couldn't stay home alone and I am sure I drove my roommates crazy with my insecurities. Anyway, long story short, a wonderful man who could see that I was not doing very well, suggested I go to therapy and get some help.

I had finally had enough and went to seek help so I could be happy and not so insecure. I was in a women's group and I started to analyze my past and why I was so insecure, depressed, and anxious. I was fascinated by my own life and focused on why I was such a mess. I was also pretty good at helping others in the group to see why they were having problems as well. Now, mind you, none of us were finding happiness, but we connected in our hope that we could change and overcome our pasts. I started to think that I was pretty good at this and maybe I wanted to become a therapist. I changed my major in graduate school and started to work in the counseling world. The longer I analyzed myself and my past, the more it looked like the cause of my unhappiness and the more hopeless I felt. I thought I was broken and I would have to manage life with this disability. My family suggested that perhaps my work was 'getting to me.' They said

'You are so angry and serious... why don't you try something less intense?' Ha! What did they know?

The funny thing was, the more I thought about my life, the more depressed, anxious, and serious I became. At first, I thought if I got to the bottom of things, I would then be able to change and be happy. But that never happened, and the more I focused on my problems or the problems of my clients, the more depressed I got, the more serious life looked to me, and the more I thought I needed to focus on the seriousness of life. I was unable to see how to find my health and happiness. About six years into working as a therapist, I started to see that there was something missing in the work that I was doing. I could see that I was not happy, my colleagues were not happy, and my clients were not happy. I was still afraid of being home alone, and my relationships with men had been brief, so finding happiness in marriage didn't look possible. I began to think that therapy and counseling were a waste of time. I thought about killing myself; I thought I was doomed to anxiety and depression. I remember thinking, 'I just want to be happy,' and felt confused as to why that never happened.

Two weeks later, I went to lunch with a colleague who had just returned from a trip to listen to a man talk about a new way of looking at psychology. He said that he was starting to work from this perspective and it was working well for his clients, as well as for him. Interesting, but it sounded too weird for me. I was not interested... but there was training coming up and my colleague told me I should attend if I wanted to learn more. Now, I didn't really think there was anything to learn, but I did think that maybe a psychology conference might be a better place to meet men than clubs or parties. I really wanted to find someone to love me, marry me, and then I would be happy, so I thought, what the heck, I will go and see what this new thing is about.

The first week in December of 1980, I showed up late, tired, and burned out. I sat in the audience and asked a million argumentative questions. I was very serious about the man saying that we should be positive, since to me that meant we weren't getting at what was deep and sick in people. I remember saying, 'Women are abused in this world. That is not just a thought!' I could feel my forehead tighten between my eyes as I tried to figure out what he was trying to say. I thought that he was talking so far over my head that I couldn't intellectually grasp what he was explaining.

I returned for the afternoon session feeling better and was intrigued by what he was talking about. So, I went back and started listening – instead of thinking and arguing. I wasn't so serious and all of a sudden, my world shifted and I awakened to the answer I had been looking for. I realized that all of my fears and problems were coming from me, not from my life. I 'saw' how thought worked to create my reality. I realized I had been looking through a filter of negative thoughts and that made my life look serious, scary, and they made me feel unhappy, anxious, and hopeless. I started to laugh as I realized I was seeing my own thoughts, memories of things that scared me, and a very vivid imagination which made the future look like the past. I realized that there was nothing wrong with me. I wasn't what I thought I was, but rather a part of something much greater and more beautiful. I started to laugh and I was filled with a beautiful feeling so powerful. I couldn't help smiling. I couldn't take life seriously from that beautiful feeling even if I tried. Everything changed from that moment because I realized I was already healthy, happy, and whole.

Now, that doesn't mean that I don't have moments when life looks scary and I need to get serious about things that need to be changed or stopped. But now I use that serious feeling as a signal that I am stressed and insecure. I know what to do about that in the present moment... quiet down and let those thoughts move on. When I look again at my life now, it doesn't seem scary and dangerous. I know that I can handle whatever life sends me because I know that my inner wisdom will come through and help me to see what to do, just as it did so many years ago.

Why Getting Stressed About an Imaginary Future is not a Good Use of our Mental Resources

Sarah McAreavey

Life can be pretty messy at times, and we can often spend time in wishful thinking around wanting to change our circumstances, thinking that events have to work a certain way for us to feel okay. Taking things one step at a time as life unfolds, is all we can ever really do. A trip back from a French holiday helped me see this even more deeply and provided some very insightful learning.

So, we were coming to the end of a fabulous holiday in the south of France with extended family. My parents had already packed up and left our villa, and were casually waiting for us to join them at a café we knew in the local town.

I was chatting in the kitchen with my brother and his girlfriend and was about to lock up and leave the villa too, when my husband, Brian, announced he needed one last trip to the toilet. We then waited for what seemed like a long time for him, and were all getting impatient as we wanted to get on our way to meet my parents, and then journey north through France to Dieppe to catch our ferry in three days' time. Some minutes passed and still no Brian, so I decided to check the bathrooms, but there was no sign of him. Confused, I decided to check the car. The kids were already waiting in the car, and so was Brian! I was fuming. He'd managed to leave the villa without the three of us realising it, and he hadn't noticed we were inside waiting for him.

I was still fuming with him as I drove away, and I was still venting my frustration when we drove into the town centre.

I 'know' it's always a sign that I've gone off into a detached and unhelpful reality when frustrated repetition shows up in my dialogue with my husband. But my frustrated, angry and irritated feelings felt SO real, and SO like he was the cause of them. I just couldn't see through the innocent mistake we had both made in our communication, and that it really wasn't a big deal. The strength of my feelings looked like they were even more of an indicator that he was 'in the wrong', and it all felt very personal. I just wasn't able to let it go.

Driving with this level of mental interference is never a good idea, and not surprisingly my normal intuition couldn't be heard through the static of my noisy, judgemental and self-righteous thinking.

Insightful Learning 1

Never enter into important decision-making when you know you have unhelpful, rattled thinking. Your judgement will be 'off' and it often doesn't end well.

The town was busy, so finding somewhere to park near the café was proving difficult, and my stress levels were still pretty high. At one point I had to reverse out of a small car park, which was full. As I was doing so, I had a very strong sense there was a small bollard to the front right of the car, which I thought I'd spotted on the way in. It was not visible as I was reversing back, and in my continued irritation I decided to ignore my instinct, and I also assumed that if there was something there, then my car's parking sensors would pick it up.

I was wrong. It was a nice hulk of concrete, just the right shape and size to do plenty of damage to the car and the wheel, and it sounded REALLY BAD when I hit it. I got out and had a quick look and couldn't see any obvious damage, but as we drove to find a space, the dashboard indicator was telling me how rapidly the tyre was losing pressure. I just needed to park somewhere, before it was completely flat, which I did.

Straight after the accident I spent a few minutes in tears feeling very sorry for myself, going over in my head what had happened, how I wished it had happened differently, and making up future scenarios as to how I thought things were now going to play out over the coming days with such a tight schedule to drive north and catch the ferry home.

I later reflected that my struggle and upset were not about what had actually happened, but in repeatedly wishing that events and decisions had played out differently. I was also playing out a 'poor me' story of having made a mistake or failed in some way.

Insightful Learning 2

It is not possible to feel anxious when we are present to what is happening, no matter what the circumstances. We are amazingly resilient, can handle anything life throws at us, and come up with solutions when we insightfully see this.

I knew from the sound when the car hit the concrete that there was more damage than could be seen, even though everyone was trying to convince me it was just a flat tyre.

We had three days to get to Dieppe and in that moment of complete uncertainty we had so many questions: Was the car quickly repairable? If it wasn't, how would we get to the ferry in time? How were any costs going to be covered?

What was really curious for me on reflection was that my husband and I did not argue once with each other after the event, and we laughed at how different that would have been five years ago. There was no mention of the misunderstanding at the villa or my misjudgement on parking the car. Our focus was now entirely on 'What now?'

Insightful Learning 3

It models great psychological health when kids see their parents pull together as a team in a crisis. It is easy to be fooled into thinking that an uncomfortable feeling can come from another person when we are feeling in a bad way. I recall my parents frequently going into 'blame' mode whenever something unfortunate happened on holiday, which I think is very typical of most couples.

French culture is very different to British and getting anyone to take action or make any decisions quickly seemed incredibly frustrating at times. It took five hours to get the car collected by the tow truck. My husband made and received fifty-plus phone calls that day to and from the relevant insurance company and garages, who were supposed to be helping us, but with zero progress!

The garage in Bergerac where the car ended up never actually assessed the car in the three weeks it stayed there, long after we'd left France.

Insightful Learning 4

It really helps your sanity to know you don't have to control outcomes to feel okay. It is a lot less tiring and energy-sapping too. It can make room for a few laughs and lightness in what can look like very grave circumstances.

The promised fast roadside assistance 'onward journey transport' did not materialise and they could not even provide a hire car that day. So, after hours of more phone calls and lack of action by our breakdown recovery company, we took the brave decision to take a taxi to our pre-booked hotel for the night. We would then drive the next day to catch our ferry home (only now it would be in a hire car).

The taxi bill to Tours came to €910. We didn't really know if the insurance company would foot the bill, and we still had no confirmation as to what was going to happen with our car, but handed over the fee in cash (which we'd had to get out from a few visits to different ATM machines en-route), laughing incredulously at the situation we found ourselves in.

Insightful Learning 5

Money can't make you feel anything, but is commonly misunderstood as being able to give us lots of feelings, both good and bad. It's a useful tool and a means of exchange, that's it. Seeing that so clearly enabled us to make a very quick, stress-free decision to pay the taxi driver to go where we needed to be with very limited alternative choices.

We all found the four-hour taxi journey surprisingly fun, and were in great spirits, even though there was still a lot of uncertainty at play. We arrived in Tours that evening and stepped straight out of the taxi and into a nearby restaurant, where we had the most simple but delicious meal. It reminded me of how different our experience of food can be too, depending on how present we are when we eat.

At this point in our journey, we still had no definite confirmation that the car would be returned to the UK to be fixed, which our UK dealership garage said we should push for. There was a very real possibility that I might have to stay behind in France, go back to Bergerac and manage getting the car fixed, and then come home alone. The kids were upset at the thought of that happening, and so was I. But I was also the only one that could stay in France and still work, whilst everyone else needed to get back for work or school.

Insightful Learning 6

I was totally okay with the children being upset at the thought of me staying behind, and I was also pretty upset at that thought too. I felt no need to get them to change their emotional state, or tell them to feel a different way, or to suppress my own emotions. We don't need to be scared of our feelings when we know they aren't telling us about how dire our circumstances may be, but are a very clear indicator of where our thought is taking us in that very moment. That is why we can feel down when we are in a beautiful place and those around us are having a great time, or we can feel joyful and laugh when circumstances look very grave.

We made it to Dieppe and caught the ferry in time. It ended the holiday like something out of the end of a movie. The large ferry ramp door opened to a beautiful sunset as we arrived back in England after such trial and adversity, all together, without the car or luggage we went with, only a small rucksack each, but hugely happy and grateful to be on home soil again. My husband turned to me at the end of the three days and said 'I know it sounds strange, but I've really enjoyed spending the last three days with you,' and I said 'Me too.'

Insightful Learning 7

We can always feel truly connected to our loved ones, no matter what is going on, when we understand that it is thought alone that creates our moment-to-moment experience.

I recall a couple of days after returning home walking down the street with Brian in the sunshine, feeling so happy and carefree and yet still not knowing when the car would return from France. We managed easily without a car for a month. The car was repatriated and fixed at our local garage, and the whole bill including the huge taxi charge was picked up by our insurance.

They were such a memorable three days, which in some very strange way, made the holiday even more special. We survived adversity whilst laughing a lot, seeing our own in-built resilience and surviving such extremes of emotions, none the worse for it.

We All Play Dress-up

Jacquie Forde

I woke up and felt awful. My head was pounding and my throat felt as though someone had been quietly sandpapering my uvula. Typical, isn't it? When you have something important that you dare not miss, this happens. I was ill.

Today was no ordinary day. I was meeting with senior staff at the Ministry of Defence to talk about wellbeing. Not the kind of wellbeing they are used to talking about. I wasn't going to discuss band-aid wellbeing. You know the kind that only focuses on the outside of your body such as massages and spa days. Great as they are, they are only ever a temporary fix. I was excited to talk with them about innate wellbeing. The kind of wellbeing we all have deep within us, but no one really talks about.

This was an incredibly important day for me. I had not long started my coaching and training company and word was spreading about the work I was doing in the community and privately with clients, helping people manage their mindset and their mental wellbeing. I didn't want to mess up or be unclear in my communications. I felt so strongly about wanting to make a difference to the people I had the opportunity to work with and I knew with every fibre of my being I could do great things to help them with the personnel issues they were having.

So – despite feeling awful – I got up, showered and dressed, making sure to wear my most professional business suit. After all, I was meeting with senior officials and I wanted to look the part. My head was still pounding but my throat felt easier after sipping some hot tea so I was good to go.

When I arrived at the Ministry of Defence, they asked me to wait in the reception area. It was incredibly busy with all sorts of people coming and going so I was delighted to have a chance to people-watch as I waited.

My appointment was for 10.30 a.m. and as always I had arrived early.

I was actually quite content to simply wait to be collected once they were ready to take me to their offices, but an hour went by. My head was pounding and my throat began to ache again.

I felt terrible and noticed my mood becoming darker and darker. I became unsettled and quite angry that they had left me so long with no word of why they were running late.

I tried to settle myself and found that no one could give me any information about what was happening. People were passing me by with most of them dressed as civilians in their most wonderful business attire. It was 90 minutes and counting and still no one showed up to collect me. By this time my mood was so dark and I was incredibly fed up and annoyed.

I looked up and found myself all of a sudden surrounded by military personnel. They all looked immaculate. Their boots were shiny, their brass buttons gleamed in the daylight. They looked strong, determined, on purpose and the guns they were carrying scared me. I found myself taking a sharp intake of breath. I had never been in this kind of situation before, surrounded by gun-wielding military personnel and to be honest I really didn't like how it made me feel. My breathing got faster. I became red in the face and my heart was pounding in my chest.

Frightening thoughts filled my mind and the feeling state I found myself in was incredibly unpleasant. I tried to calm myself, to breathe deeply, but none of it worked. I don't think I have ever felt so unwell with my mind spinning out of control.

Then as quickly as I had gotten myself into this anxious state, a fresh thought appeared. It was a gentle whisper, so quiet that I almost missed it.

'Bless them,' it said. 'They are only playing dress-up.'

I started to giggle. This thought was so true. The men in uniform carrying their guns were simply playing dress-up. The same way I had put on my suit that morning and the same way we all played dress-up when we were little children. Only then it seemed fun, carefree and light and yet I had lost sight of that light-heartedness in a moment of seriousness.

In my lowered state of mind, which was worsened by not feeling well, my mind had gone crazy thinking up all sorts of various scenarios about the men in uniform. So much so that I had scared myself.

That day taught me so much about the incredible power of our personal minds to create stories.

Through stories, we share passions, sadness, hardships and joys. We share meaning and purpose. Stories are the common ground that allow people to communicate, overcoming our defences and our differences. Stories allow us to understand ourselves better and to find our commonality with others. Yet stories within our own minds can also hold us back, limit us and stop us from evolving because we believe that memory to be true for us now, even though it might not be.

Can you think of a story you have held in your own mind for a very long time and then realised it was no longer true for you? I have lost count of how many times I have found my own narrative to be no longer true for me or for those I love.

In the meantime, until more of these stories reveal themselves, I am going to enjoy watching myself and others play and no longer be scared of my own internal chatter.

After all, we all play dress-up, don't we?

Our True Nature Transforms the Status Quo

Julieanne Chazotte

Status quo—The existing state of affairs, especially regarding social or political issues. (Oxford Languages)

The status quo can look as though it's difficult to change. In reality though, it isn't. It's effortless, because it's imaginary to begin with.

Our existing state of affairs is made of human thought. Lots and lots of human thought. Thought that started generations and generations ago in many cases. But the good news is that thought isn't who we are and it isn't fixed. It's not concrete, and by nature it's changeable.

What doesn't change though is truth. Truth just is, and there's something more true about all of us that has nothing to do with the ephemeral nature of the status quo. This deeper truth has to do with what's most fundamental about us and it's more powerful than anything we could possibly make up using the creative power of thought.

If we step outside of the status quo for just a moment, we may find ourselves asking, 'What occurs to me to say or do when I see beyond what has become known as "normal"? What occurs to me when I'm inspired by the innocence, purity and goodness of my heart and of my soul?'

If we reminisce, we most likely all have memories that remind us that what is known as 'normal' isn't a given and it isn't hard to see through or beyond.

For me, one memory like this had to do with getting my first full-time job as a waitress. I was eighteen and for some reason I knew like the air I breathed that people had goodness in them. I knew that we could change things for the better by bringing out the best in each other rather than the worst. I also saw that not many people around me seemed to think like this, yet I still knew it was true. I knew there was a certain type of alchemy available to us if we would come from love.

I decided to run an experiment to see if this was true.

Normally when the restaurant was busy, each individual would struggle to take care of their own section of tables. We would all just keep our heads down, get things done and make it through until the storm passed. We would each come out with our own 'war stories' of how something had gone awry and a table had been really pissed off by it all.

One day it occurred to me that this seemingly 'normal' experience didn't need to be this way. I realized that there was a certain magic we could tap into that would change it all. It occurred to me that I could help my co-workers take care of their tables in ways that were hard for them. So that night during the rush, I looked for little things I could do that would make a huge difference. If water needed to be filled, I filled it. If a table was looking for ketchup or extra silverware, I got it for them. I did this for as many people as I reasonably could and it all flowed from a feeling of goodness.

I wondered if doing this would have any real impact. I found out that it did. What happened next felt like watching a miracle unfold.

Little by little my co-workers started helping each other out without me ever having said a word. It was like watching energy and intention shift right in front of my eyes.

Through a simple act, and a beautiful feeling, the culture of the restaurant changed from one of barely making it through and every man out for themselves to one of teamwork, generosity and people looking out for each other. It completely changed the tone, mood and way in which we worked together for the remainder of the evening.

While I knew this simple experiment had very big implications and have replicated it in various ways since, I was reminded this year how much I had lost sight of the power it showed me. After George Floyd was murdered and protests broke out worldwide, I saw that I had fallen asleep and bought into an unconscious narrative that made it look as though the status quo was more fixed than it actually is.

Somewhere along the way, it had stopped occurring to me that love, hope, possibility and goodwill are powerful and can inspire change in ways the brain will never understand.

I felt jolted awake during that time and, as I listened and engaged with life and with others over the next few months, inspiration started to flow with this reawakened Spirit. It was amazing to watch others wake up as well and to see what was emerging and changing.

A group of us came together and created something we thought could help in shifting the status quo within our own community.

The story of this awakening is of course still writing itself. We will not know all the ways in which things will change/not change in the days and years ahead, but I think it's incredibly valuable to slow down, value even the simplest examples of change to see where true change comes from.

So how do humans go from creating the existing state of affairs to a healthier state of affairs?

The times when I have watched powerful change occur, I have noticed that wisdom, peace, love and understanding have been at the heart of it all.

This has been true whether it was something simple like the waitressing story I shared above, or something truly epic like the changes that occurred during the American civil rights movement that Martin Luther King Jr helped lead in the 1950s and 60s.

Regardless of what type of change one is interested in, it seems that love and true understanding is the power that helps transform the status quo for the better.

Another memory that comes to mind for me around this took place after I graduated from my master's program in education. I was teaching high-school English, and I was so excited! I knew the power that education and a caring environment could have on a teenager's life and I was passionate about providing that experience to my students.

My first year though, I wasn't really prepared in some funda-mental ways. I was young and didn't understand the importance of loving classroom management. I taught in a charter school where the kids faced some really challenging circumstances, both personally and societally, and in many cases the students I was working with were giving high school a second chance.

I thought caring meant being their friends. I didn't understand the need for structure and leadership, and so my classroom was often chaotic and occasionally fights would break out. I would often take my prep period to cry some tears and pick myself up before the next class.

Over time, however, I started to see what was needed. I was fortunate enough to have some incredible mentors and I made use of them! I asked as many questions as I could, reflected on what happened each day, and tried something new to see if it would make a difference.

By my third year of teaching, I had a much deeper understand-ing of what helped to create a healthy environment where the students could feel safe, let their guard down, and be engaged in their learning.

One thing that occurred to me was that from a feeling of respect and goodwill, which is natural to us all, we could talk together about creating a healthy environment where everyone could thrive.

I started the conversation by asking them a seemingly simple question, 'Do you want to feel safe in this classroom?' Unsur-prisingly to me by this point, the answer was unanimous, 'Yes!'

It didn't matter whether the student was a 'good student' or a 'challenged student,' in a gang or not in a gang. Everyone agreed. They wanted to feel safe.

They were settled and safe enough to answer the question to begin with, which was a feat in itself. By answering it, layers and layers of coping skills and conditioning had been quieted for us to be able to ask something so fundamental.

We spoke about what that would mean, what that would require of us, how we would need to treat one another, and how we would need to take responsibility for our behavior. We also spoke about being safe to mess up. I told them there might be days when I was having a bad day and that I'd like them to let me know if I wasn't living up to our agreements. We were all equals in this, all in the same boat, all coming from the same source of truth.

We ended these conversations with a shared understanding and a deep respect for one another.

This may seem like a small thing to some but, that year, no fights broke out in my room, and students who were members of different gangs were able to learn side by side in the same class.

I think this memory comes to me often because it points to something I deeply believe and think will be a teacher for me for the rest of my life—there is a fundamental goodness in people that can create a level of change that the intellect will never understand.

Prior to that year in teaching, I knew on a deep level that humans deserve respect because each of us is created from the same source. In essence, we are one being, and yet we have a mind. While our minds can create many different thought-created realities, the essence of who we are is always there, always ready to emerge.

And the truth of this wasn't realized in my class until it was. I could have gone on thinking that the status quo was for it to be challenging for students to behave and impossible for us to really get along. I knew that wasn't true though. I knew there was something much more true than that.

It makes me wonder, what is possible for society if we are able to see more clearly the power that love, wisdom and understanding truly have?

I know the unhealthy parts of our existing state of affairs can change. Underneath the fearful thought and conditioning that has created the current status quo, there is a True Self, ready and waiting to be expressed. It's a really beautiful, magnificent thing. Instead of creating from the existing conditioning, fear and insecurity, we would create from greater levels of wellbeing.

The norms in society that create harm for some and make it easier for others are created with thought, and the good news is that thought can be changed. It's this deeper truth about humans that's unchanging.

And while change doesn't have to be hard, it does require us. It requires our hearts, our souls, our wisdom, our insight, our passion, and hopefully the joy we have, simply for being alive.

And that doesn't mean it won't be painful at times. It can be quite painful to wake up from who we thought we were. Yet the awe-inspiring quality of our True Nature and natural goodwill can lift us up when we are lucky enough to see their impact.

If we want to change things, one thing I know to be true, is that we need to see truth even more clearly than we do now. That's what makes the difference. The truth already is, and inspiration and wisdom for change come from there.

Your Own Picture

Jan Armstrong

On the face of it, life on Earth for humans is a pretty grim scenario. In the background there is a continuous drama unfolding: people fighting each other for land or for peace or for God; there's the poverty gap, pandemics, health statistics, political shenanigans, human rights, animal rights, pollution, ecocide and extinctions. I'm sure we all can add to the list.

The middle-ground isn't much better; looking to ourselves and our families, we never have enough money or time, we get divorced, we are unwell mentally and physically, overweight, codependent, abused and, since Covid, there's a whole raft of new negatives to deal with.

Close up, horror of horrors, look at me, I'm not good enough, not pretty enough, not clever enough, not man enough, a bad mother, suicidal, alcoholic, addicted, anxious, depressed, anorexic, agoraphobic, bulimic, bipolar, schizophrenic.

A very serious situation, you must agree. So much suffering. What on earth are we going to do?

This picture is the one I had hanging on my wall for the first sixty-five years of my life. I took it all inside, absorbed it, and became full up with it. I was suffering at all levels. Life shouldn't be like this. Why don't people see? I also believed the media propaganda about appearance and lifestyle and I fell short in every way. I literally hated what I saw in the mirror.

In my middle years, unwell in both body and mind, struggling to cope and not realising that what I was experiencing was a spiritual emergency, I sought solutions to my mental and physical distress. I met a kind, wise man, who opened me to my first glimmer of understanding. He specialised in the spine; at the end of my treatment, he said to me 'Jan, where do you live?' So I told him my address, and he smiled and explained to me what he meant. 'This is where you live,' he said, and put my hand on my heart.

That was the first crack in my shell, I remember it clearly: I caught a glimpse that day of the answer that was already there but which was still buried within. I was not ready yet to change the picture.

I worried constantly, not conscious of the fact that the future is a figment of imagination, and I lived fearfully in the land of 'what if?' My heavy thinking was creating my fear, and my fear was creating my mental illness, which was manifesting in my body. I worried about everything – the next moment and the big picture. What am I going to do? How can I be happy in a world where people fight each other for peace and appear to be unaware of the direction in which it is headed? I felt simultaneously impotent and responsible; I was isolated mentally, physically and spiritually. I became ill. I struggled emotionally with constant fear and anger, and the energetic dissonance that I felt as a result of living my life in a world that didn't feel right. It manifested as illness in my mind, my heart and my gut.

Bodies are programmed to thrive and survive, and symptoms are the evidence of the healing process. Our bodies experience fear (and peace and joy) through biochemical messages that are activated in the brain, but which originate in the feelings in the heart and mind which are generated by our thoughts.

The first thing that happened was that I began to shallow-breathe which resulted in panic attacks, and my body misunderstood and thought I was in danger all the time. After a while my diaphragm and my nervous system ceased to function as they should and I became unable to breathe healthily. I misunderstood the symptoms which resulted from my body's biochemical response and I sought ways to fix them. It is exhausting and damaging when the fight or flight responses are activated constantly by our anxious thinking – they are designed for extreme focused energy so that we can escape physical danger (like sabre-tooth tigers).

My solution of choice was alcohol, which I discovered early in my career as a worrier, and I embraced it as an ally which damped down the anxiety which increased as my physical symptoms increased. They were chronic at first, irritable bowel syndrome (IBS) and fibromyalgia, very limiting, especially in conjunction with my mental symptoms of anorexia and agoraphobia. The doctors did their best to treat the symptoms with their pharmaceuticals, many of which turned out to be addictive and involved serious withdrawal problems. Eventually I became acutely ill when my heart malfunctioned and I found myself in hospital having an emergency pacemaker inserted.

I believe that it is usual for momentum for change to build up gradually; of course, epiphanies do happen, but I still suspect that a crack will have been opening up prior to those moments. Anyway, I continued on my Way of the Victim for decades more, until finally, in my mid-sixties, I found the solution, the golden key that had eluded me throughout all those years.

I learned that I am not just a hapless character in the play of human life; I am the author of my own story. I always have a choice in how I experience whatever happens to me, however overwhelming the circumstances may seem; the key is that it is me who is thinking up my reality. I can paint the canvas of my mind in colours that are either dark or bright, and out of the raw materials of the world of form, I can create a reality that is either tragic or comic, or simply beautiful. I had misunderstood my joy and fear – they are not *caused* by an object or an event, but by how I *think about* what I am experiencing, whether it is a happy day out or a turbulent flight. Between myself and my experience is always a thought.

William Shakespeare knew this in the sixteenth century when Hamlet, knowing that he is a prisoner of his own thoughts, says *'there is nothing either good or bad, but thinking makes it so'*. Many of Shakespeare's characters experience the misery of madness because they misunderstand the power of their thoughts and believe scenarios that are not true.

This realisation was the turning point for me. I came to understand that thoughts are impulses passing through me from the divine energy of the universe. They are not truths or instructions – they are my own creative tools. I can pick them up and use them or discard them and the way I know which ones to trust is in the way they feel. If they feel light and clean and clear, then those are the beneficial ones. Gradually, as I stopped giving credence to my uncomfortable thoughts, although my outside world hadn't changed, everything within me felt different and my life became easier. My constant fear began to lift and as it did, my health improved.

Habitually taking our thinking seriously weighs us down and prevents us from accessing our natural wisdom. We believe that certain feelings are good, others bad; these beliefs cause us to suffer. Letting go of rigid beliefs leaves space in our minds and hearts for light to come in and bring fresh new ideas and realisations.

I saw this truth one day in my sixty-fifth year when I stopped drinking. The insight appeared to come out of the blue, but of course the foundations had been building in my subconscious ever since I first saw the power of thought. In the moment that I reached for my habitual drink, I realised that my addiction wasn't a thing, it was a belief. I had built it out of a complex portfolio of outdated ways of thinking, now no longer valid. I had painted myself into a picture of dependency and worthlessness and, in that moment, the old thinking was painted over by the new. I understood my 'need' as a construction of my mind. I was free after forty-five years and it had taken just one new thought to release me.

Parallel to my discovery that I create my own life experience, I have realised that the workings of the Universe are not mine to comprehend or solve. My feelings are the light and shade and texture of my human life which is the only life I can experience and influence. All thought and all life is transient. Happiness and seriousness are not fixed – everything is subjective and impermanent; our thoughts and feelings change of their own accord, like clouds covering the sun on an April day.

I know now that the only thing that always remains firm is love. It is the light in my heart, the ground of my being, my anchor to the rock from which I build all the imaginary castles of my fascinating and glorious life. It is the essence of Life. So, step out of your darkness and know that you hold the magic wand of creation. You alone paint your own picture: so use all the colours and don't take it too seriously.

Is the Climate Crisis 'Serious?'

Ami Chen Mills-Naim

I've had trouble writing this essay. For a few years now, I've been exhorting people in my spheres to become *more serious* about the global climate and extinction crises. I don't mean 'serious' as in emotionally serious, but rather, intellectually serious, like, *real-world* serious. Serious, as in: This is actually happening, folks.

Some of my colleagues in the spiritual-psychological worlds I inhabit do not believe in such ideas as 'spiritual bypass.' I understand this sentiment. We do not want to, nor should we (!) wallow in our negative thoughts and bad feelings. Where does this get us?

But there is a difference between wallowing and simply not being *afraid of our feelings*. There is a difference between pretending all is well and *telling the truth.*

I believe spiritual bypass exists. For me, spiritual bypass is a way our intellect diverts us (via spiritual platitudes) from accepting the reality of something that may be painful or feel overwhelming. The spouse is cheating on us. We pretend this is not happening. The child is being abused. We refuse to acknowledge this. Thus, the cheating continues and the abuse continues.

For me, spirituality is not about residing in one's 'happy place' at all times. Spirituality includes courage and a deep, loving embrace of the whole world—including its actual, darker realities and the profound suffering of the human and other species.

When we acknowledge and accept 'outer reality,' wisdom is freed to respond within us and through us with right action. We confront the spouse. We protect the child from the abuser. Nothing about these actions is non-spiritual. They are, indeed, *deeply spiritual* because they are founded in love—in a deep respect for oneself, for the 'other' and for life itself.

In The Three Principles (3P) world, our mantra is to *'listen for a [positive] feeling.'* This speaks—rightly—of the nature and tone of insight and spiritual revelation. This phrase also speaks to the severe limits of the intellect in providing spiritual-emotional relief and awareness, which is a function of the heart and soul, or 'Universal Mind' in 3P parlance.

But this exhortation, for me, does not mean we do not understand that 'bad things' happen in the world of form—events, world and community leaders, politics, and economics that hurt people physically, threaten democracy and even, now, civilization as we know it.

For many years, I cared about climate change—in a distant way. But it was not until the spring of 2019, when I traveled to Kauai with my husband, after a separation, that the climate crisis became more real and immediate to me.

I need to backtrack, however, and tell you about the sea stars. My children and I—when they were young—used to visit a spot by the sea in Northern California called Mitchell's Cove. We squatted by tidepools and poked at purple anemones and ochre sea stars (often called 'starfish').

One year, the sea stars began to fall apart, disintegrating before my eyes. I did some research and discovered this was due to a disease, exacerbated by a warm ocean 'blob'—a marine event that has become more prevalent as the oceans absorb atmospheric heat. When the sea stars did not return, I did more research, and discovered that kelp beds along the California coast were also disappearing. Because sea stars had died, sea urchins were exploding and urchins were eating kelp at a manic pace. We were losing the 'forests' of the seas that support so many other species. Indeed, by the time I looked into it, bull kelp beds were 90% gone in California.

Fast-forward to 2019 and my favorite place on this green planet, where I was, with my husband, re-newly in love. Kauai was and always is paradise, a jagged, breathtaking emerald swath of nature's tropical bounty, seemingly eternal. Out of the blue, I received a text from an old friend. The text included a link—to corporate sustainability professor Jem Bendell's now viral paper, 'Deep Adaptation,' (2020 revised edition) written at the University of Cumbria in England.

What can I tell you about this paper? It is thirty-five pages long, including extensive footnotes. The paper is about the state of Earth, how far gone we are, and how psychologically challenging it is for humans to wrap their minds around the probable demise of the planet, or rather, of a fully habitable planet and the natural systems we rely on to live.

Bendell—in a sober, kind and respectful tone—referenced multiple 'feedback loops' of global heating that humans, by their emissions, are triggering around the globe. A warming planet releases more greenhouse gases from natural systems, and thereby heats *even faster*.

Because CO_2 remains in the atmosphere for a hundred years and more, we are 'locked into' a certain amount of global heating already. Bendell's conclusion is that 'social collapse' is possible, probable and perhaps inevitable, as food systems are impacted, and many areas of the world become uninhabitable. Unlike scientists with the IPCC*—which has been challenged from many quarters as overly conservative—Bendell (2020) suggests we are in a state of collective denial about the fix we are in. And, as Sydney Banks has also said: *'Denial is not a healthy state.'*

Already, massive wildfires, extreme droughts and huge storms are creating conditions for collapse. When? Bendell prefers not to guess, but when pressed, he allows, maybe within ten years in many parts of the world.

When I got home, I followed up with my own research, as a former journalist. It was all true. Melting ice and snow releases methane from the Arctic permafrost; and now methane, a gas with twenty to a hundred times the heating capacity of CO_2, is 'leaking' out of earth and seas in Arctic regions. A darkening Arctic (because of the disappearance of white, reflective snow

---

IPCC: Intergovernmental Panel on Climate Change, the highly esteemed United Nations group convened to study and predict the causes and effects of climate change and global heating.

and ice) absorbs more heat, an effect known as 'albedo.' There was more... about the oceans and forests: their capacities for absorbing any more heat and CO_2 dwindling rapidly — eventually oceans, even rainforests, will turn on us, and heat us, too.

But ultimately, we have turned on ourselves.

I accepted Bendell's analysis, with wiggle room for possible miracles, rapid shifts in human consciousness and resulting behavior change and, perhaps—I allow, with trepidation—careful uses of technology that might help. There is more to climate and caring for Earth, however, than just CO_2 in the atmosphere. Our fixation on 'endless growth' and worship of technology has led us to the 'Sixth Mass Extinction of Species'—the result of a heating biosphere, deforestation, ecosystem degradation, and human-generated waste and toxins everywhere—in oceans, fresh water and on land.

So, how can any of this relate to being less serious?

Over the last couple years, I have realized that the enormity of what we are facing is actually what prevents many of us from facing it. That is, the 'seriousness' we may slide into (rather, perhaps: panic, fear, anger, anxiety, even despair) is what keeps much of the world population trying not to actually look.

I myself went through a period of deep sadness and mourning, then anger and anxiety, then action around climate. I have friends and colleagues in the 3P world who have done the same.... In the end—and this is the hard part—the antidote to 'seriousness' or despair around climate is acceptance. As usual.

Acceptance ('yes, it's happening') frees the mind to clear; thoughts of resistance to what is clear out. Situations like the climate and extinction crises become more obvious and impersonal to us. There is more to see with a clear mind, including: cause and effect, how we got here and perhaps how we might get out.

From clarity of mind, we gain the bigger picture. Humanity has always been full of horrors. We have been killing, and enslaving and exploiting each other since nearly the dawn of human history. Human stupidity, greed, ego and insecurity are surely no surprise.

And Earth, after all, is a speck, an atom within a speck, really, in the swirling, unfathomable entity we call 'universe,' and now, even *'polyverse.'* If life on Earth falters, the universe goes on. *Life, God, Mind* is so vast as to be beyond all measure and comprehension. Even if all species die here, Life IS.

There is great sadness, tremendous tragedy, in the loss of biodiversity, in the loss of the unique beauty and intelligence of each insect, fish, amphibian and furry mammal that disappears—and, of course, in the loss and suffering of humans now and to come.

Yet and still, the energy of life, even as 'forms' die or transform, does not find a part of itself missing. Once, Mr Banks was asked a question about reincarnation and 'would we come back to Earth?' Surprising me, Mr Banks said: *'Why would it be Earth?'*

So, Life is much larger than what we experience here. In total, it cannot be hurt. We do not have that kind of power. We are not, in the end, more powerful than God.

I say these things, but it took me over a year to understand more deeply these spiritual truths. I could repeat them more easily, more blithely before I understood the facts.

I found it very challenging to face the 'end of the world' as we know it within my lifetime, and more so, within my children's. I would be surprised if anyone, no matter how spiritually enlightened, did not feel some feelings around what we have done to our home, to our beloved Mother Earth.

But with acceptance, finally, comes a sense of deeper peace, a re-connection to our oneness with All and essential wholeness. From this peace, we may, according to our personalities and skills, decide to step up to the plate and act. This action then comes from a deep and natural impulse and, most importantly, it is non-attached.

We may hope for an outcome, but the actions themselves are simply happening, almost of their own accord. And our personal wellbeing is not contingent on what happens next. Because we are already connected to wellbeing, even on a faltering planet.

As we explore our innate wellbeing in light of the demise of ecosystems, and *our own personal temptations* to stray from it (via judging and attacking others, attacking ourselves, attacking government, the fossil fuel industry, runaway capitalists, etc.) we become more genuinely useful. I do not mean we might not *call out and exert tremendous pressure* on some of these groups in order to effect mass change. I mean: We do not need to live in anger and judgment.

When we begin to dissolve personal thoughts about how things are, and how they shouldn't be, a wiser, more effective form of thought flows in: insight, right action, compassion, and importantly, a continued joy in living. After all, there is much to en-*joy*, still!

Then, we don't have to think so much, we just do as we feel, from the heart. I, for example, have become very politically active in the US—advocating for protecting our democracy and protesting, lobbying and speaking up about climate and species extinction.

But beneath all of that is a deep silence, a wonder at nature, the fresh air, the spring buds, the power of the sea. When people ask why I do what I do in politics, I say: *Because I feel like it!*

Rather than look for answers to such questions outside of yourself, you can trust your own feelings. Insight and wisdom come in with a feeling—of rightness, wholeness and healing. This capacity to discern is in you and with you.

As the spiritual teacher Gangaji often says: *'Tell the truth.'* What may at first seem frightening and uncomfortable, in the end, is freedom. Once free, we can be used in unexpected ways in unafraid service to Life.

The Gift of Travel

Juliet Fay

Hilariously, writing this chapter has been an exercise in taking things too seriously. Initially I was drawn to the topic of seriousness. There are so many occasions where seriousness has robbed me of joy, weighed heavily on me and created all sorts of unnecessary difficulties, stress and suffering: the perfect topic. I could say so much but then choosing what to write got tricky.

I could write about the impact of seriousness in: love, sex, relationships, parenting, work, activism, spirituality, friendships, food, writing or exercise. Then I realised there is one area where seriousness has been largely and notably absent: travel. From the age of twelve I was enthralled by the idea of travelling to foreign lands. I devoured stories of Victorian female explorers. These exotic creatures were few and far between, but I sought out their tales and thrilled to their adventures. The freedom I sensed fascinated me. These fearless women, driven by the desire to go beyond the confines of their culture and upbringing, spoke to something deep within me.

Sure enough, I began to travel. By luck, good fortune and steeped in privilege, invisible to me, I found foreign trips came my way. I stayed with French and Spanish families in my early teens, attended gatherings as a Girl Guide in Switzerland and Sicily, as I reached sweet sixteen, then took off to India and Nepal, a fresh-faced school-leaver. I was spellbound by the sounds, sights, smells and spirituality of these wholly different cultures and landscapes. Living as if I were somebody else, entirely comfortable as the eager, curious (and hopefully respectful) visitor, I felt so alive, so utterly absorbed by this glorious, high-definition present. My travels yielded a never-ending supply of new experiences. Though there were moments of illness, homesickness and no doubt boredom, frustration and loneliness, they seemed of little consequence, when my senses were so drenched in the new and the wonderful. By contrast, life in my hometown seemed small and dull yet oddly I also returned with a sense of affection though no desire to linger there for a moment longer than necessary.

I knew very little about what I wanted to do or be, what career I might pursue. I couldn't settle on anything. There were so many options, how could I choose? But I knew I wanted to travel. To have more and more of these wonderful, thrilling experiences. Why would I not? I returned from Asia unsure about higher education but willing to give it a try (lucky me, I had a place at university waiting for me). That first summer, Italy called again and four of us spent a month interrailing up and down the boot-shaped country I'd grown to love. Eating, laughing, sunbathing, revelling in each other and our adventures.

Before long, another opportunity to feed my insatiable appetite for travel appeared in the form of a chance to study in Italy for six months. All funded by the (no longer available to UK citizens) Erasmus scheme. I couldn't believe my luck. There were disasters and difficulties to be sure, but like a great film these just added texture and comedy, blending seamlessly with the beautiful memories. The delight of growing fluency in another language, soaking up the architecture of Bologna, my senses waking up to the literature, food, fashion, loves, newfound friends, visits from old friends and family, day trips, just hanging out, celebrating my twenty-first birthday in Venice. It was like a dream.

One thing was missing: a fellow adventurer. He showed up when I was temping in London after a fond farewell to Italy. I was still twenty-one. There followed several years of adventures in Papua New Guinea, Australia, Solomon Islands and Vanuatu. Peppered with triumphs and disasters, just like any other year but the joy of the new continued to permeate, as a wonderful, pulsing background to the daily round.

A return to the UK saw travel mostly halted for fifteen years as we set about raising organic vegetables, children and turning a small farm in Wales to organic poultry production. A brief return to Italy to attend the Slow Food Terra Madre conference in Turin in the early noughties was a delicious reminder of the utter delight of steeping myself in new places and experiences, far from my everyday experience. Somewhere deep inside, I knew my travelling days weren't done, but opportunities to get away looked like they belonged to another life. One I wasn't living.

An unexpected trip to Malta in 2013, visiting the place my grandfather had lived, opened the doors again to that yearning to explore. The following year my personal life changed irrevocably. While travel had remained uncomplicated, adored and easy, most other things in my life had become unbearably hard. Mostly my inner life which was often stressed, tormented and wildly unpredictable.

Fast-forward two years, I was living alone and got the opportunity to take two of my children to visit old friends in Nairobi, Kenya, where my parents lived in the 1960s. Like learning to ride a bike again, after an absence of many years, I quickly got my travel legs back and got permission for extended leave from my employer. We set off for a ten-day adventure visiting Nairobi, travelling the Mombasa highway and spending a few nights hearing lions roar in the distance in a game park. My daughter had never been on a plane. I was thrilled to travel again and witness my children's experience.

Since then, travel has returned to my life, like a beloved old friend. The company (or lack of company), place or activities mattered less than the happening of it. A package holiday to Bulgaria, learning to ski for the first time, was no less a high point than house-sitting on a mountain in Greece for a month one Christmas. Through it all, the highs and lows continued, sometimes with periods of introspection, even depression, but the aliveness I was chasing, still looked to be found in a ticket away from home.

North America, never really high on my list of places to visit, became a frequent destination prior to the pandemic. First Vancouver and Salt Spring Island, Canada, then California, Oregon and Washington State. I seem to have left my heart (with a special someone) in San Francisco!

And so, what has this to do with seriousness? In this enjoyable revisiting of my travels, I recognise how easy (mostly) travel has been for me regardless of my finances, work situation or personal situation. Easy, uncomplicated, loved and appreciated. Not true of many other areas of my life. Of course, it looked like it was travelling that gave me that openness, curiosity, expectant delight – and travel that fed the desire to feel more alive.

Through 2020 and the early months of 2021, while international travel has been largely suspended, I've come to realise the aliveness I so often felt then was not caused by travelling (though of course it looked to be so, absolutely). The aliveness, the not taking things too seriously, was a state, allowing a more unfiltered experience of life. In contrast: how much effort, judgement, difficulty, insecurity, straining and controlling has attended so many other things in my life?

Work at times, relationships over many years and most of all myself. Boy, have I taken myself seriously. It has led to much suffering for me and others. What if that freedom of mind did not depend on doing something you love or being somewhere you love or even being with someone you love, but was in fact, what remains, when the self-criticism, judgement, doubt and insecurity fall away?

I had no clue at the time that this might be what was going on. What if that freedom of mind was available any place, any time? What if the grinding, reactivity, unease, pushing boulders uphill was not in the end about the job, the relationship, the business, the climate, social injustice. Not in fact, about anything out there, but simply a mind-created confinement that sucks the joy out of life, leaving it flat, monochrome and dull or on fire when our low-level anxiety blows up into attack or defence. Do I mean we could live joyfully regardless of circumstance? Not exactly. What it looks like, is we can see life from a different viewing platform.

One that is not concerned primarily with how this event, place, person or thing affects our multi-layered, contradictory sense of ourselves. Rather we become receptors: life flowing through us as it may, fully alive to the joys and sorrows, highs and lows, but less of it sticking. In short to become present to our moment-to-moment experience.

It turns out I have been present to so many moments, but unaware that I was. Seriousness is a great clue. We notice those serious times. They feel constrained, yucky and heavy. But perhaps what we don't notice, maybe can't notice, is the absence of seriousness. We're too busy living at those times. More of that please.

Lessons From the Creation of This Book

When I started to put this book together, I had no idea of how to do it or where this journey would lead and still don't, but I felt compelled to create it anyway.

The creation of this book has been an ongoing lesson in taking my thinking less seriously:

- ✿ In being led by my soul and not my head and seeing where that leads...

- ✿ In coming up against my habitual 'I'm going to get into trouble' fearful thinking and not getting stuck in that...

- ✿ In waiting for how to best respond to people from a neutral place rather than an uncomfortable, loaded place...

- ✿ In getting beyond my insecurities and self-created 'comfort zone' and contacting people with an open mind, unattached by the outcome...

- ✿ In coming up against myself over and over again whatever 'myself' is in that moment...

- ✿ In juggling my life as a mother, a wife, an employee, a volunteer, with being the creator of this book...

✧ In listening to my body screaming at me to slow down and focus on the day-to-day before I can continue with all the other demands of time and attention...

✧ In trusting that the words and required actions will come when they are ready and no amount of thinking about them is going to bring them forth more quickly...

✧ In knowing when to go back to sleep and knowing when to get up to write...

✧ In hearing my negative self-talk and recognising that I am my own worst enemy when I constantly berate myself for the smallest misdemeanours...

✧ In not being OK when sometimes I am a bit of a scatterbrain...

✧ In pursuing what I hope will make a difference to people and the world even when that seems insignificant to what is required...

✧ In learning to get beyond my desperate need to please everyone and not to unintentionally upset them...

✧ In seeing I have no idea how others view me...

✧ In seeing time and time and time again I am not in control...

✧ In creating space in my life for doing something that lights me up ...

- ☼ In having the courage to share my light/my truth with the world...

- ☼ In knowing I have everything I need ....

- ☼ In trusting myself...

- ☼ In following my star...

- ☼ In following the path of love and connection...

- ☼ In just being...

I wish you a life less serious.

George Halfin - Editor

Questions and Reflections

» Did you notice any common themes that run through the stories even though each story is different?

» Which story resonated with you the most and why?

» Have you experienced any insights similar to those expressed in the book? And if so, in what areas of your life?

» As you read the stories, did you notice your feelings changing and becoming lighter or less serious? If so, why do you think that happened?

» Can you think of an event or situation which seemed like a terrible thing at the time but turned out to be fine or even positive in hindsight? The event did not change, so what shifted your perspective?

» What if any thoughts do you think you take seriously regarding your relationship:
  • to yourself
  • to others
  • to the world?

» What if anything did you see differently about your life in any of these areas from reading this book?

» What thoughts did you have about yourself that held you back in your life? How do those look to you now?

» If you could ask any of the contributors anything, what would it be?

» Would you like to experience less seriousness in your life and learn more about what the contributors have seen that has helped them?

Find out more

To access more resources (including supplementary videos by contributors), carry on the conversation and find out about our events, go to:
alifelessserious.club

Jan Armstrong: Jan lives in Suffolk and shares her life with her two adult children and two grandchildren. She has self-published two books of poetry and a small travelogue about Greece. Her writing reflects the influence of the work of the late Sydney Banks upon her. She considers life to be a gift from which we are able to create anything we choose; everything we need is already within us and our task is to trust and allow ourselves and others to find and follow our own path towards personal and planetary health.

© Dida G. Heilmann

Ivalo A. Arnfjord: Ivalo lives in Greenland with her husband Steven and their two children. She has a Master of Arts in education and is a PhD student specialising in play. In 2018 she created a Greenlandic Three Principles Facebook group with her friends; it now has more than 3,500 members. After training with Mette Louise Holland from 3P Instituttet Denmark, she now coaches and gives courses about The Three Principles. She is passionate about early childhood education and care and people accessing their innate health via The Three Principles.

Liliana Bellini: Liliana is an experienced Three Principles facilitator who has touched many lives with the depth and love she brings in her teachings. From CEOs, prisoners and housewives to the homeless and teenagers on the edge of crime, Liliana has helped all kinds of people discover their innate potential to lead fulfilling and happy lives.

She is co-founder and co-director of The Big Simple, a new social enterprise dedicated to helping young adults who are going through the care system.

Before her work in The Three Principles, Liliana worked for fifteen years in the field of complementary medicine. She is married and has four grown-up children.

Carol Boroughs: Carol is a Three Principles facilitator and mentor working in the field of personal transformation. Carol guides people as they wake up to their true nature and signposts the way to a deep sense of inner peace and wellbeing. When someone uncovers this deep sense of wellbeing, their lives begin to transform.

Carol shares The Three Principles with a diverse range of people of all ages and backgrounds around the world and offers mentoring to people at all stages on the spiritual path. Her work is deeply rooted in the knowledge that The Three Principles provide a unique and powerful understanding of our true nature which can help us uncover our unlimited potential for peace of mind, compassion and love.

© Adam Lewis

Julieanne Chazotte: Julieanne is a life and business coach who guides and supports individuals and businesses to navigate life with greater ease. She points people away from the habits that create stress, pressure and sometimes burnout and towards what naturally allows them to access better-quality thinking, creativity and momentum.

She is also a co-founder of SimpleSHIFT, a platform based on The Three Principles understanding, whose mission it is to help people create more health, wellbeing and ease across all areas of life and the way we do business.

With master's degrees in education and in spiritual psychology, Julieanne brings over eighteen years of experience in the field of education and coaching to each person, project and company she works with.

Ami Chen Mills-Naim: Ami is a former investigative journalist and current essayist, global speaker, author, coach, teacher, and podcast and radio show host. She is also a wife and mother of two, based in Northern California. In 2019, she helped found her local Extinction Rebellion (XR) chapter, was one of the organisers of the massive climate strike that year and served in the Regenerative Cultures Working Group for XR Global Support. For the last five years, she has dedicated herself to bringing the 'spiritual', 'political' and ecological worlds together. She is currently writing a book on this subject.

Kate Dalgliesh: Kate lives in Somerset with her husband and their three teenage children. Kate came across The Three Principles and the teachings of Sydney Banks and experienced a huge shift and transformation in her own life. Feeling the truth and magnitude of this message, she now works sharing this understanding in the hope of bringing more joy to those who listen and hear within.

Angela Dawson: Angela is a Bristol-based flash memoir writer and postmenopausal married mother of three. She wild writes with intimate circles of midlife women. In this tender space they listen, write, speak their naked truths and bear witness. Together they reawaken, liberate and reclaim their instinctual soul voices.

Tania Elfersy: Tania is a transformative coach and award-winning author, specialising in midlife women's health. She has spent years researching what causes and what can relieve the emotional and physical symptoms associated with perimenopause and menopause. She became free of her own range of symptoms, naturally and simply, through insight alone.

Tania set up The Wiser Woman project in 2015 to help women transform their experience of midlife change. Through her coaching, writing and teaching, Tania focuses on connecting women to the innate brilliance of their bodies, having seen that healing occurs with ease when we relax into the divine intelligence within. Her clients have witnessed their symptoms disappear and the unfolding of a greater sense of wellbeing, all without having to 'fix' their hormones or change their lifestyle.

Jenny Elleray: With over fifteen years dedicated to teaching and studying The Three Principles around the world, Jen has developed her own unique voice for sharing this one simple truth. Her clear and heart-felt teaching resonates with her audience, whether at a large conference, in a small group or individually. Her own transformation, moving beyond shyness, depression and eating disorders, continues to inspire her to point others to what can happen when they see the true nature of themselves and life.

'No matter where it is in the world, no matter what the external conditions people are living in, these universal truths or principles speak to human beings enabling them to wake up to how life really works. I am passionate to be able to share in whatever way I can, and help others to do so too.'

Karen Evanoff: Karen, from rural Alaska, is of Dena'ina Athabascan descent. With a life experience growing up in nature and academic degrees in counseling and cultural anthropology, her work revolves around documentation, preservation and revitalization of ancient Indigenous practices and earth-based values. From a holistic approach, she specializes in educational project and programme development. She recently started a new business that offers rural Alaskan retreats and land-based activities including hiking, kayaking and renewing natural world connections. She fully believes that the bridge between humans and earth is a vital part of transformative health and wellbeing for all.

Lara Fares: Lara was born in Lebanon, grew up in France and has been living in London since 1998.

As a mother of four, her own spiritual journey has been deeply rooted in family life, giving her a deep passion for helping others, particularly young people, to live their best lives. Over the years she has studied with many of the world's leading spiritual teachers and forged her own path towards spiritual understanding and evolution.

Lara describes her true calling as helping people to remember that they are worthy and special, offering hope to those who have lost their way. She hosts various private spiritual and personal development groups bringing together teachers from around the world to share with people from all walks of life.

Juliet Fay: Juliet is a poet and facilitator working with organisations and individuals interested in accessing more wellbeing, clarity, creativity and joy in life and work. She offers training workshops, facilitates gatherings, and creates poetry, illustration, artwork and prose to stir the heart.

Jacquie Forde: Jacquie is a gifted teacher, coach and intuitive based in Scotland with a thriving global practice. She brings a spirited personality and vivacious, humorous attitude to her work as a coach and mentor. Jacquie is passionate about sharing her knowledge and allowing her clients the space to embrace their own innate wisdom to tap into their highest potential to build their businesses and improve their lives.

Christine Friend: Christine has spent the last fifteen years helping her clients to reduce anxiety and create a life and relationships they love.

She is naturally drawn to helping young people and parents who are struggling and is a lead facilitator with iHeart, teaching 10 to 21-year-olds emotional resilience in schools and universities. She works online and in person with clients from all over the world coaching, mentoring and public speaking.

'I love to show people the simple secrets to having less on their minds; and revealing what is currently invisible to them – but available to everyone that wants more fun, play and ease in their lives.'

Farah Halabi: Farah is a Transformational Life Coach who helps her stressed-out, overwhelmed and overstretched clients uncover their innate awesomeness and God-given gifts to lead a life of insightful wisdom and peace. Farah is certified in the Science of the Nafs Psychology which is the Quranic science of the self. She serves professional Muslim women and supports them to overcome the challenges that prevent them from being the Muslimah* they want to be, and guides them to create the life they want, to live a life they love.

Muslim women.

© LeviLily Photography

George Halfin: George is an Innate Health coach, project manager at a national UK charity and mum of two. With Farah Halabi she is co-chair of Ni-sa-Nashim Essence (part of Nisa-Nashim – a national network which brings Jewish and Muslim women together across the UK to inspire and lead social change) and runs wellbeing sessions for their members. She is an Associate of Unstoppable!, a Three Principles career and coaching business, as well as author of the blog 'Confessions of an Overthinker' and contributor to the book, *From the Heart: Explorations in True Nature and Unconditional Love.* She is passionate about supporting people to see beyond their preconceived limitations for themselves and the good of society.

Christine Heath: Christine is a licensed Marriage and Family Therapist and Master Addictions Counselor. Her passion is helping people to realise that they are able to recover their health after any trauma or mental distress.

She was personally mentored by Sydney Banks for more than twenty-five years and has more than forty years of experience providing Three Principles based therapy, supervision and training. She is a founding member of The Three Principles Global Community. She works internationally providing training, consultancy and coaching to anyone that wants to awaken to the power of this understanding.

Christine has been the Executive Director of the Hawaii Counseling and Education Center since 1985. It is the longest operating Principles-based mental health and outpatient addiction programme in the world.

Christine is co-author of *The Secret of Love: Unlock the Mystery, Unleash the Magic* and currently co-hosts a podcast, 'Psychology Has it Backwards', with Judy Sedgeman.

Elaine Hilides: Elaine is a Three Principles trainer and coach, a number one Amazon author, and international speaker and online course creator. Elaine was introduced to this paradigm in 2009 and promptly jettisoned everything she had trained in before then, including NLP, TFT and hypnotherapy. She also tells terrible jokes.

Elaine works in many different fields including addiction, weight loss and mental health, and is passionate about them all. *'Why should I niche,'* she says, *'when everything is underpinned by thought?'*

Elizabeth Lovius: Elizabeth is a changemaker: a board-level leadership coach and mentor, social entrepreneur, author and poet who supports leaders to access their own wisdom, liberating their purpose, potential and performance. Elizabeth has worked with over 10,000 people in all business sectors and is particularly passionate about women leaders living a heart and soul-led life, listening to their innate wisdom and challenging the business world to change the game and balance their focus on profit with attending to people and the planet.

In 2011, she came across an inner game-changing understanding – which transformed her own life, her work and her vision for the world. Since then, she writes, teaches, podcasts and runs workshops on living and leading from your Inner Core and is often inspired for the joy of it to write poetry that speaks beyond the intellect to our heart and soul.

Susan Marmot: Susan works with people from a wide variety of sectors. She is the co-founder and co-director of a social enterprise called The Big Simple (CIC) which works with young disadvantaged adults, especially those exiting the care system.

She is also a facilitator on The Slice of Happiness programmes, sharing The Three Principles with those dealing with mental health issues, and helping people in prison discover who they are and who they can be when they are not caught up in their usual thinking.

Previously Susan has been a trainer of practitioners on the faculty of the One Thought foundations programme. She also specialises in working with couples to help them have happier, more contented relationships.

Sarah McAreavey: Sarah is a transformational coach. She runs a busy practice sharing her years of knowledge gained from extensive training in health and nutrition, and the psychology of health and wellbeing.

Sarah's particular interest has always been focused on the mind-body connection, recognising the importance of how we create our experience from our state of mind and how this affects the body's physiology. This groundbreaking approach helps her clients declutter and quieten their minds to tap into their own powerful intuition and healing, whilst pointing them towards greater peace of mind and wellbeing in all areas of their lives.

© Frances Dale

Sue Pankiewicz: After years of self-help attempts searching for answers whilst overthinking her life and relationships, Sue discovered the work of Sydney Banks in 2005. This led to year-long facilitator training with Dr Roger Mills and several opportunities to learn from Mr Banks in person.

Learning about the principles behind the 'human operating system' revealed that the only thing that had ever stood between Sue and her longed-for life was wonderfully simple. Best of all was naturally rediscovering fun, light-heartedness and freedom.

For the past sixteen years Sue has shared this understanding widely in diverse settings including teaching and mentoring individuals and groups, hosting home-based retreats, and introducing The Three Principles in schools to pupils and staff.

Along with her business partner and friend Sheela Masand she launched The Viva Event in 2015, an annual, much-loved, international event held in Spain.

Linda Ramus: *'We are all students, we are all teachers.'* Operating from this paradigm for over twenty years, Linda, as both a student and facilitator of The Three Principles based services, has experienced the mystery and magic of sharing this understanding with an amazing diversity of individuals from at-risk communities to the human services professionals who served them.

Upon retiring from Santa Clara County in 2012, she founded Transformative Research and Consulting with the goal of providing evaluation and research support for Principles-based programmes. Not willing to let this be an abstraction, until the pandemic, she continued to facilitate and learn from weekly classes where she never ceased to be amazed and humbled by the magic of a simple insight. Based in Fremont, California, you will also find her lugging her backpack up and down wilderness trails and on caminos in Spain.

Janet Rhynie: Janet is a woman with an infectious laugh, a passion for life and stepping outside the box. She lives her own mission statement to educate, elevate and liberate her mind to live a life yet imagined and her life and work as a coach and part-time probation officer inspires others to do the same.

Having spent more than twenty-five years in the field of personal development and behavioural change, she knows the experiences she has had in her life are here to assist others. That is why her programme, Rediscover You After Divorce, was born out of her own self-rediscovery journey after divorce.

© *Dwayne Josephs*

Lucy Sheffield: Lucy is a magical writing coach, children's fantasy author and intuitive abstract artist. She has published two books, co-written two books and helped others to publish their work.

On a day-to-day basis, Lucy helps female professionals go from being under-confident writers to published authors, step by step via her eight-month programme, helping them to find their own unique voice and share this with the world.

Lucy has always had a passion for creativity. She expresses this through her love of writing and art. Lucy helps female professionals to find their own unique voice and share their message with the world through writing their book. In her spare time she loves to express through her art work.

Debra Simmons: Debra is a Wisdom teacher, relationship expert and a lover of the magic of money. She has written two books and runs a successful business called Dare2bu. Right now, Debra is on a mission to help 1,000 courageous women find financial freedom and a mind that supports them to enjoy it.

Debra has always had a passion for walking her talk and living the wisdom and magic she shares with others. She loves to help the people she works with find their own unique gifts and live a great life from ease, love and peace.

'We all crave the knowing of ourselves. Yet we often lack the courage and daring to look past what we think we know to find the magic that lies dormant inside. Once awakened we can never go back and life becomes a true adventure, with all the thrills and spills of a great story unfolding with passion and brilliance. Yet our hearts are full and overflow with love, gratitude and the truth of who we are.'

Bronwen Warner: Bronwen is a perfectly imperfect human mum of two daughters, aspiring writer, children's physiotherapist and mental health practitioner whose practice is based on The Three Principles philosophy.

She is passionate about supporting women and children to create lives that make their heart sing, no matter what has happened before or what happens next. Bron considers herself a fellow life explorer and loving cheerleader embarking with people on a magical, transformative journey back to who we really are.

References

Banks, Sydney (no date) Audio recording – 'The Best of Two Worlds', in 'Sydney Banks: A Collection of Four Vintage Recordings', International Human Relations Consultants, Inc., https://3pgc.org/product/sydney-banks-a-collection-of-four-vintage-recordings/

Banks, Sydney (1998) *The Missing Link*, International Human Relations Consultants, Inc.

Bendell, Jem (2020) 'Deep Adaptation: A Map for Navigating Climate Tragedy', IFLAS Occasional Paper 2, Revised 2nd edition, https://www.lifeworth.com/deepadaptation.pdf

Criado Perez, Caroline (2020) *Invisible Women: Exposing Data Bias in a World Designed for Men,* Vintage.

Dickinson, Emily (1891) '"Hope" is the thing with feathers', in Franklin, R. W. (ed.) (1999) *The Poems of Emily Dickinson*, Harvard University Press.

Hay, Louise (1984) *You Can Heal Your Life,* Hay House.

Holland, Mette Louise (2017) *Dit selvhelbredende sind: Introduktion til din medfødte sundhed*, audio version, Lindhardt og Ringhof.

Packer, Toni (2007) *The Light of Discovery,* Shambhala.

Pransky, George (2014) *The Relationship Handbook: A Simple Guide to Satisfying Relationships,* Pransky & Associates.

Robinson, Mary (2019) *Climate Justice: A Man-Made Problem with A Feminist Solution*, Bloomsbury.

Schuller, Robert H. (1984) *Tough Times Never Last, But Tough People Do!*, Bantam Books.

Source disputed between Albert Einstein, John A. Shedd and Grace Hopper according to quoteinvestigator.com

Steinem, Gloria (1971) 'The New Egalitarian Lifestyle', *New York Times*, 26 August 1971.

Sydney Banks resources

You will find resources by Sydney Banks including recordings, books and videos on the following websites:

- sydbanks.com – which was set up by his publishers
- sydneybanks.org – which includes his personal biography and reflections
- 3pgc.org – The Three Principles Global Community, where you can find newly edited Sydney Banks videos and a wealth of other Three Principles related information and resources

Acknowledgements

This has been a soul-led project like no other, which started with an idea of what I wanted to do and who I would contact from the many amazing women I have met on my journey of learning about The Three Principles. The project then took on a life of its own where each conversation led to another, some with women I knew, some with those I didn't. I enjoyed and got so much from each conversation that I wanted to continue having them forever – but then realised I had enough for the book so had to stop myself.

To all the amazing women who took time and effort to contribute to the book, thank you from the bottom of my heart for your contributions and your sisterhood. For those I never got to speak to, you are in my heart and I know that you have many more stories to tell.

To Carol Boroughs and Lucy Sheffield, my amazing editing team, thank you from the bottom of my heart for your support, your encouragement, your time and your wisdom.

Thank you to Cathy Presland, Allan Boroughs, Jacquie Moses, Chetna Bhatt and Ellis for your support, encouragement and advice in the early stages of the project.

Thanks to Lydia from Thoughts Make Things for being able to encapsulate the essence of the book in your wonderful illustrations. It was my dream to work with you on this and I'm so glad I did. Thanks also to Rachel Nixon from Accuracy Matters for your excellent proofreading, your counsel, expertise and encouragement – you really helped to spur me on. Thanks to Alexa from The Book Refinery for enabling the contents of the book to reflect the cover and for your knowledge, advice and support in the final stages of getting the book ready.

Thanks also to One Solution, Michael Neill and Amir Karkouti for the generosity of content you put out during lockdown which ignited my passion for creating this book and encouraged me to pursue it.

To Ami Chen Mills-Naim, for mentoring me and for continually broadening my horizons.

To our kitten Juno, thanks for jumping on my keyboard when I needed a break.

To my kids, thanks for all your enthusiasm for this book and giving Mummy the time to work on it. I learn from you every day.

For my gorgeous husband Matt, thank you for giving me the space for this to be my thing whilst still supporting me from the sidelines with your encouragement and support looking after the kids even more than usual when I needed you to.

And finally, thank you for taking the time to read it.

Printed in Great Britain
by Amazon

77703868R00121